WRESTLING'S GREATEST STORIES

Inside Stories about Cage Matches, Royal Rumbles, Smackdowns & Wrestlemania

Colin Burnett

OVER TIME BOOKS

© 2008 by OverTime Books

First printed in 2008 10 9 8 7 6 5 4 3 2 1

Printed in Canada

The Publisher: OverTime Books is an imprint of Éditions de la Montagne Verte

Library and Archives Canada Cataloguing in Publication

Burnett, Colin

Wrestling's greatest stories / Colin Burnett.

ISBN 10: 1-897277-14-8

ISBN 13: 978-1-897277-14-0

1. Wrestling matches. 2. Wrestling—History. I. Title.

GV1196.25.B87   796.81209   C2007-906176-1

Project Director: J. Alexander Poulton

Editor: Brian Crane

Cover Image: Shawn Michaels and Steve Austin, Courtesy of Corbis; UP955271

PC: 5

Contents

Introduction 5

Chapter 1:
A Brief History of Wrestling 9

Chapter 2:
**The Irresistible Force,
The Immoveable Object** 29

Chapter 3:
The Rivalry 49

Chapter 4:
A Flair for the Gold 69

Chapter 5:
Home Is Where The Hart Is 89

Chapter 6:
To Hell and Back 109

Chapter 7:
A Tribute Gripped By Tragedy 128

Chapter 8:
Glory Bound? 144

Notes on Sources 167

Dedication

To "Granddad" Dawes, without whom four succeeding generations of Dawes' would never have developed a taste for 'rasslin.

Introduction

Every wrestling fan has an opinion about wrestling's greatest matches. This wrestling addict grew up in Canada in the '80s admiring performers like Ric Flair, "Macho Man" Randy Savage and just about any villainous fiend hatching a plan to put an end to Hulkamania. So I have views and, sadly, biases of my own.

Many matches are solid contenders for the greatest of all time. Some are familiar, some less so. Fans of the World Wrestling Federation (WWF), now World Wrestling Entertainment (WWE), often champion Randy Savage vs. Ricky Steamboat at *WrestleMania III* as the best they have ever seen. They also hold the 1997 Hell in a Cell match pitting Shawn Michaels against The Undertaker in high esteem. Then there's Steve Austin vs. The

Rock at *WrestleMania X7*, perhaps the greatest *WrestleMania* main event bout ever. Fans of junior heavyweight wrestling with an international flavor cherish such scorchers as the 1991 World Championship Wrestling (WCW) series between Brian Pillman and Jushin "Thunder" Liger, or the high-flying Extreme Championship Wrestling (ECW) television title bouts between Rob Van Dam and Jerry Lynn. Others favor the prestigious New Japan Pro Wrestling Super J-Cup final where Chris "Wild Pegasus" Benoit defeated The Great Sasuke, or the touching best-of-three-falls draw featuring ECW's Eddie Guerrero and Dean Malenko, a true technical clinic. Diehards of hardcore action cite the vicious ECW battles between Masato Tanaka and Mike Awesome as bouts that simply cannot be missed. Experts also remind us that women have competed in some of the best contests, especially the tag team classic, Manami Toyota and Toshiyo Yamada vs. Dynamite Kansai and Mayumi Osaki, which was held at one of the best cards of wrestling action of all time, Dream Slam II on April 11, 1993. For others, the 1994–95 All-Japan Pro Wrestling tag wars pitting Kenta Kobashi and Mitsuharu Misawa vs. Akira Taue and Toshiaki Kawada remain the showstoppers to top all other showstoppers. Each of these titanic battles is essential viewing for any serious fan.

Yet, none of the classics I mentioned above made the cut for this volume. So what makes a great match great? What qualifies as a 5-star battle? Is it the match that goes over the 20-minute mark? One that makes the crowd red-hot? Does there have to be a great finish and a definitive winner? Does a major title have to be on the line?

There are many reasons for admitting a given match into the pantheon, but for better or worse, I tend to favor matches from the WWF/WWE. So the National Wrestling Alliance (NWA), the American Wrestling Association (AWA), ECW, not to mention many worthy Japanese promotions are all underrepresented in the pages that follow. Hopefully the reader will overlook my many blind spots and appreciate reading about the matches that I have chosen.

What follows are not my choices of the seven greatest matches of all time. They're just a sample of superb battles that casual wrestling fans will enjoy reading about for the first time and the committed expert will take pleasure in reliving. Some matches are selected because of their quality or historical significance. Others are here because of the behind-the-scenes stories and on-camera storylines.

No truly great match exists in a vacuum. For this reason, I try to give the reader a sense of the impact these matches have on the private and professional lives of the wrestlers who partici-pated in them. Hulk Hogan's long journey to the top, A.J. Styles' fight to find steady work and Ric Flair's battles with management, these personal struggles often echo battles waged in front of cameras in unique ways and vice versa.

Now more than ever, the world of wrestling seems to be less about wrestling than about the attractions that surround it: the scantily clad, buxom women, the backstage antics, the lengthy "promos," and even the movie advertisements. Wrestlers—so the promoters would have us believe—are entertainers. But some fans remain nostalgic for the bygone age of rasslin' with its smoky, dimly lit arenas and performers known more for their hairy backs and inarticulate snarls than for their athleticism and witty "stick work." One element ties that earlier age with today's multi-million dollar industry: the great matches. Wrestling's greatest brawls, "spot fests" and technical clinics—the exciting stories told in the ring, as well as those that unfold behind the curtain—is what this book is all about.

Chapter One

A Brief History of Wrestling

The names Hulk Hogan, The Rock, Ric Flair, HHH, Sting and the Ultimate Warrior all conjure up memories of some of wrestling's best matches and storylines. There's Hogan's memorable steel cage match against "Mr. Wonderful" Paul Orndorff on a 1986 edition of *Saturday Night's Main Event*, in which the match, eventually won by Hogan, had to be restarted midway through because both Hogan and Orndorff hit the floor at the same time. There's the Ultimate Warrior's scintillating 28-second victory over the Honky Tonk Man at the first ever *SummerSlam* in 1988, a victory that saw the Warrior end Honky's almost 15-month title reign (a record that stands to this day). And there's the almost yearlong buildup to Sting's encounter with then baddie Hollywood Hulk Hogan at *WCW Starrcade '97*, in which Sting, playing a silent character reminiscent of *The Crow*, dropped from the rafters of arenas around the country to save hapless victims of the dreaded heel faction, the nWo.

Very few of the people who watch those matches today think that they were real. Not even young children. Clearly, they were all carefully (and sometimes, not so carefully) planned out move for move and the interviews setting them up painstakingly memorized and rehearsed. The storylines surrounding them were clearly plotted out in detail months in advance. Watching these matches, it's hard to imagine that anyone ever believed that wrestling wasn't "fake." But it is only recently—in the last decade or so—that wrestling companies have openly acknowledged the planning that goes into what they now call "the sports entertainment business" that so many of us have grown up loving.

But it hasn't always been this way.

The first pro wrestling matches seem to have taken place just after the end of the American Civil War in 1865. A wrestling fan at that time couldn't sit in the comfort of his home or in luxury seats in a $200 million arena to watch his favorite wrestler. He'd have to catch the traveling carnivals as they popped into town. These carnivals, often set up on the outskirts of town, would have a special tent erected for wrestling. Unlike today, the spectator's physical interaction in the show was a crucial part of the act.

Today, barriers separate fans from the wrestlers. But in the first few decades of wrestling, spectators were actually encouraged to test their mettle against the touring champion. Often a cash prize was offered to any local who could defeat the champ or last a set number of minutes in the ring without being pinned. These carnivals were havens for gamblers, hustlers, petty swindlers and money-grubbers. What kept wrestling afloat as a carnival attraction in these years was the money made from bets on the side.

But the promoters of the day—the Vince McMahons of the era—obviously didn't want to lose the money they'd put up for the bets. So they would do whatever they could to ensure that their wrestler didn't lose. They'd even put carnival employees in the audience disguised as ordinary fans. These "plants," as they were called, rehearsed with the wrestler before the show. Plants would wrestle the champion, win the match and collect the payoff, seemingly exposing the champion as a pushover. Word spread around town that the wrestler was cinch to beat, thus encouraging local tough guys to take a crack at him and make some easy money.

Unfortunately, any wrestler worth his salt was cutthroat, talented and always at the top of his game. In other words, he wasn't a pushover at all. Once the toughest townsfolk climbed into the ring, the champion had what it took to win the battle.

These early matches were violent and stiff. With large sums of money at stake, the wrestlers couldn't afford to make mistakes. They avoided the flailing fisticuffs of their overconfident foes and mat-wrestled them into submission. By the time the townsfolk realized that they had been swindled and figured out how much money they'd lost, the carnival was well on its way to the next town.

Eventually, people in the crowds began to catch on, and to survive, wrestlers like "The Iowa Cornstalk" Fred Grubmier actually started swindling the swindlers. He would travel around pretending to be a local yokel, challenging carnival wrestlers and betting on the match. He'd pin the far less talented carnival wrestler in short order and win a pot of loot.

At the same time, in major towns and cities, bars and saloons began hosting wrestling matches. Each bar had its own roster of wrestlers. To keep things running smoothly, the fighters agreed behind the scenes to avoid seriously injuring one another during matches.

But promoters weren't going to be outdone, and as wrestling grew in popularity, they realized there was money to be made from performers who had star appeal or a unique appearance or an impressive physical ability, especially when they were show-cased in a series of matches. This is how wrestling storylines were born. It is also when fixing and planning matches became most important. To keep a feud going, each wrestler needed to win a few and lose a few. The promoters who set the stage for the wrestlers' epic battles had figured out that the wrestling matches that would etch themselves into fan's memories, that would grip them and excite the simplest and most visceral emotions, that would get them to buy tickets and come back for more, needed to be fixed. Properly handled, a series could have fans screaming at a big payoff match.

The most notable early wrestling feud on record is the series of matches between Frank Gotch and George "The Russian Lion" Hackenschmidt in the early 1900s. At the time Gotch was a major sports hero and the American heavyweight champion. Hackenschmidt was wrestling's first ever recognized world heavyweight champion, a title that some fans say can be linked to the NWA world title held by Ric Flair in the 1980s. Their April 3, 1908, bout was one of the most important sports events of the year because the winner would hold both the world and American titles, unifying them for the first time in history. Gotch defeated Hackenschmidt in an amazing two-hour and three-minute, best-of-three-falls marathon match (best-of-three-falls matches were the norm at the time) and became a household name—the era's Hulk Hogan.

Drawing a record crowd of 28,000 fans and generating a massive $87,000 box office, the rematch on September 4, 1911, was wrestling's first mega-event. But what fans at the time didn't know is that it would also be wrestling's first high-profile double-cross! The promoters' plan was to split the first two pins and take the bout to three, making it seem the two feuding wrestlers were perfectly matched. But the enormously adored Gotch knew that The Russian Lion had been injured going into the bout. (Some even go so far as to say that Gotch paid a trainer to give Hackenschmidt the injury.) With the largest crowd in the history of wrestling watching, Gotch ditched the plan and pinned his weakened opponent in two straight falls. Gotch's hand was raised, and he took home the title again, making himself look more impressive than any wrestler in history. And all this at the expense of Hackenschmidt's reputation.

Gotch was not the last wrestler who would take advantage of opportunities like this.

As wrestling boomed in the 1920s, the fear of double-crosses loomed large. So promoters' placed the world title on wrestlers in top physical condition who could fend off any unexpected swerves in the ring. The top star of the era was Ed "Strangler" Lewis, who was in reality a talented shoot fighter. But he also understood that fans wanted to be entertained. So in a groundbreaking bout, Lewis dropped the world title to the ultra-popular football player Wayne Munn on January 8, 1925.

Their match was a box office goldmine, and Munn became an instant wrestling star. More importantly, the bout set a moneymaking formula that promoters would use over and over again through the decades. Many sports stars have followed in Munn's footsteps, including boxing legend Muhammad Ali (who fought Japanese wrestling star Antonio Inoki in 1976) and NFL stars like William "The Refrigerator" Perry (at *WrestleMania II*) and Lawrence "L.T." Taylor (at *WrestleMania XI*). And who could forget NBA bad boy Dennis Rodman's appearance alongside Hulk Hogan at *WCW Bash at the Beach 1998* or Mike Tyson's shocking pull-apart brawl with Steve Austin that same year?

Promoters soon realized, however, that handing over the title to a non-wrestler was risky because they could not be counted on to fight off the double-cross. Munn, for example, soon found himself in the ring with Stanislaus Zbyszko, who worked for a different promoter. He whipped Munn's hide so badly that the in-ring official was forced to award the match and the title to Zbyszko. This was not part of the script. Unscripted finishes like this led to many disputes amongst promoters and the creation of many world titles, none of which could claim supremacy.

In fact, the NWA—in the 1980s a league synony-mous with Ric Flair and the Four Horsemen—was put together in 1948 to curb in-ring double-crosses and to create one unified world heavyweight championship. The biggest draw in wrestling at the time was a submission wrestler named Lou Thesz, whose name is familiar to most wrestling fans today for a move that bears his name: The Thesz Press. Today it is used by former six-time WWE champion, "Stone Cold" Steve Austin. Thesz is considered by many to be the greatest wrestler ever to compete. He was certainly one of the greatest drawing cards in history and had many high-profile scuffles.

Born to a Greco-Roman wrestler from Poland, Thesz was a "hooker," a master of truly excruciating submission holds and ways to escape them. He was trained by former three-time Olympic wrestler George Tragos, who once broke a man's arm so horribly that it had to be amputated. The youngest wrestler to ever be world champion, there probably never has been nor will there ever be a more highly skilled submission grappler-turned-pro wrestler. When he won his first world title in 1937 at the ripe age of 21, Thesz became a monster star across America.

Thesz was at his best between November 1949 and March 1956, when he reigned as NWA champion. He wrestled some 3000 matches as world champion during this period. This number is extraordinary. Today's wrestlers, if they remain healthy, wrestle only 200 to 250 matches per year. Thesz wrestled almost twice as many!

Thesz defended his title all over the world, becoming wrestling's first international superstar. His showdown with Baron Michele Leone, a title unification match (Leone was recognized as a world champion in California), was attended by 25,256 fans at Los Angeles' Gilmore Fields and drew a then record gate of $103,277. His first title defense in the Orient in October 1957, a classic one-hour draw against Japanese legend Rikidozan, pulled in 30,000 fans and earned an 87.5 television rating, forever making Thesz a legend in Japanese wrestling history.

Behind the scenes, Thesz lived the life of a world champion as well, paving the way for the likes of Ric Flair, the "wheelin,' dealin,' kiss-stealin,' limousine-ridin' son of a gun" and former 16-time world titleholder. Thesz loved the money, the fame and the women (his first two marriages imploded because of on-the-road affairs). He also liked rubbing elbows with famed actors and athletes. Amazingly, he was also a traditionalist and despised gimmick matches like tag team matches and battle royals. He famously refused to wrestle on cards featuring women wrestling.

Beginning in the '50s, while Thesz's career was in full swing, wrestling hit television screens, opening the door for a different breed of star. The new wrestlers had a talent for riling the crowd before and after the match, but between bells displayed only rudimentary wrestling skills. Wrestling became more about show than it did about skill.

Still, wrestling traditionalists refused to go down without a fight.

On July 27, 1950, Thesz lifted the AWA (Boston) world title from the flamboyant Gorgeous George, a major star of the '40s whose famed "Human Orchid" persona was a true innovation. George would prance to the ring with his long, dyed blond hair held up with gold-plated bobby pins, his *Pomp and Circumstance* entrance music, a purple spotlight and a valet spritzing his "GG" Chanel #10 perfume. George was a master crowd manipulator, drawing furious heel heat for his antics and underhanded tactics. His famous catchphrase was, "Win if you can, lose if you must, but always cheat!" Despite his loss to Thesz, George's extravagance was the wave of the future.

In the '50s, much to traditionalist Thesz's dismay, the colorful and charismatic "Nature Boy" Buddy Rogers was one of the biggest attractions. On June 30, 1961, Rogers defeated New Zealander Pat O'Connor for the NWA world title in front of 38,622 fans, a number that would remain a North American wrestling record until WWF's *The Big Event* held at Toronto's Exhibition Stadium in July 1986, which was headlined by a match between Hulk Hogan and "Mr. Wonderful" Paul Orndorff and drew 74,000 fans. In 1963, Rogers went on to become the first World Wide Wrestling Federation (later WWE) champion. Anxious to use television to create a new audience for wrestling, more and more promoters began elevating the flashiest talent and the craziest stuntmen to superstardom.

The NWA, for its part, continued to look for credibility by booking no-nonsense wrestlers, like Dory Funk, Jr., Harley Race and Terry Funk as champion in the '60s and '70s. But when the rotund future WWE Hall of Famer "The American Dream" Dusty Rhodes—known less for his mat skills than his jazzy jive-style mike work—won the NWA world title in 1979 from Harley Race, the signs were clear: wrestling was about to change. And it did, in more ways than one.

Over the next two decades, powerful wrestling promotions like the NWA, the AWA and the WWF competed with one another for national and international supremacy. While smaller, more regional splinter promotions sprung into and out of existence looking for niche audiences. Through all of this, the style of wrestling matches and the characters played by wrestlers changed dramatically.

As the WWF entered its more family-oriented *Wrestlemania*-Hulkamania era starting in January 1984, it moved away from the brutality and bloodlust of the 1970s. Matches became about larger-than-life, clean-cut superheroes defeating stereotypical, often oversized villains in comic book–style clashes. Wrestling became more about child-oriented Saturday morning cartoon shows like

Hulk Hogan's Rock 'n' Wrestling and ice cream bars bearing the names and likenesses of wrestlers. Hulk Hogan would best the Evil Russian in the name of good ol' U.S. of A. one night and overcome all odds to bodyslam a 500-pound Goliath the next. Often, these baddies were managed by Bobby "The Brain" Heenan. With this formula, the WWF became an international, multi-million dollar juggernaut that today makes movies, produces DVDs and has a record label.

Over in the NWA, "Nature Boy" Ric Flair carried the mantle of "pure wrestling" during the '80s even though he was flashier and more gifted at the mike than his NWA championship predecessors. His character combined a more adult-oriented edge. There were fast cars, late night parties and interviews laced with sexual innuendo (including references to taking each and every lady in the audience to Space Mountain, satisfaction guaranteed). In the ring, he displayed prowess with solid technical wrestling, stiff chops and marathon-caliber athleticism. Indeed, at his peak, his matches often lasted over 60 minutes. In a nod to both sides of Flair's persona, fans often referred to him as "The 60-Minute Man."

This was also the moment when wrestling turned hardcore. Fans who yearned for the days of old when wrestlers would compete in bloody, no-nonsense slugfests and who despised the sanitized cartoon world of the WWF would come to embrace the more extreme battles of smaller promotions that offered alternative wrestling action. Promoters and wrestlers began experimenting with new ways of mixing scripted competition with higher risk stunt work and violence. When Jimmy Snuka left 20,000 fans' mouths gaping at the sight of him executing his Superfly splash off the top of a steel cage onto a prone Don Muraco at Madison Square Garden in June 1982, a potent image of thrill-seeking, body-on-the-line risk taking was forever emblazoned into the minds of fans. WWF fans would have to wait until Shawn Michaels' and Razor Ramon's brutal ladder match at *WrestleMania X* 12 years later for another spectacle of this kind.

Elsewhere, wrestling matches featured skin shredding, fireball throwing and excessive bloodletting. Perpetrators included the likes of WWE Hall of Famer The Original Sheik, the fork-wielding Abdullah the Butcher and the notoriously cruel Sheepherders (later watered down in the WWF as the unhygienic marching morons, The Bushwhackers).

Overseas, a Japanese wrestler by the name of Atsushi "The Wild Thing" Onita, also dubbed the "Godfather of Garbage," launched his Frontier Martial Arts Wrestling (FMW) promotion in July 1989 and took savage juice-fests to new heights. In August 1990, Onita competed in the first no-rope Exploding Barbed Wire match, in which a wrestler making contact with the barbed cables would set off a skin-searing explosion. Onita's career peaked on May 5, 1993, in front of the 41,000 bloodthirsty punters who packed Kawasaki Baseball Stadium to watch Onita square off against former NWA champ Terry Funk in a no-rope Barbed Wire Time Bomb Death match. For this bout, a 15-minute countdown would culminate with an air raid siren announcing that one minute remained. At the end of the bout's final 60 seconds, an explosion filled the entire ring with fire and smoke engulfing the contestants. Onita was declared the victor, but he received several severe burns.

FMW spawned many imitators in Japan and North America. At least one man at the time saw the potential in this formula: Paul Heyman, known in the '80s as the dastardly cell phone-wielding manager, Paul E. Dangerously. He helped reshape Eastern Championship Wrestling to the outlaw Extreme Championship Wrestling (ECW). ECW's home base was a sweaty, ramshackle bingo hall in South Philadelphia, and its cards were innovative and popular. They combined daredevil stunts and violent, weapons-laden brawls with the athleticism of more traditional technical contests, the high-flying *Lucha Libre* (or Mexican-style) cruiserweight spot-fests with lowbrow cat fights between scantily clad women. Even if its fan base remained relatively small, ECW became a grittier, counter-cultural alternative to the multi-million dollar WCW and

WWF—wrestling's equivalent to the grunge movement.

By the mid-1990s, Eric Bischoff's Ted Turner–financed WCW had taken the top spot in the wrestling world after acquiring box office goldmine Hulk Hogan and other veteran talent and launching its ultra-lucrative nWo invasion storyline. Suddenly, WWF found itself on the ropes and playing second fiddle in the U.S. market. So Vince McMahon, Jr., the owner of the WWF, decided to inject a little ECW-style "Attitude" into his promotion. With the injection of lewdness and brutality and a red-hot promoter versus wrestler storyline that pitted corporate billionaire Vince McMahon against the renegade, bird-flipping Texan, "Stone Cold" Steve Austin, WWF's style of wrestling became more reality based, stiffer, more violent and lower brow.

The two top storylines of the '90s—the threat of an nWo takeover of WCW and the Austin-McMahon feud—filled WCW and WWE arenas worldwide, giving wrestling an anything-can-happen edge. Whether it was Scott Hall and Kevin Nash infiltrating WCW's production truck or Stone Cold steamrolling his way into Joe Louis Arena in Detroit on a Zamboni, fans didn't know what was going to happen next. Hardcore bouts found their way onto WCW and WWF programming. Last Man Standing matches, Hell in a Cell matches, TLC (tables, ladders and chairs) matches, Inferno matches—they all became the norm in this era. Crash television sent TV ratings to all-time highs and blurred the line between fiction and reality. With WWE's *Monday Night Raw* running head-to-head with *WCW Monday Nitro* in legitimate company warfare, fans knew that the stakes were high and that the ramifications of what they were seeing were very real, even if the matches remained fixed. And they loved it!

It was an exciting time as promoters became more willing to blur the lines between reality and fiction. But the gamble didn't always pay off.

In 1998, for example, the WWF introduced its Brawl For All contest. WWF promoters wanted to use the Brawl to distinguish their product from the low-impact wrestling style of over-the-hill WCW main-eventers like Flair, Hogan, "Rowdy" Roddy Piper and "Macho Man" Randy Savage. This ill-advised series saw "fake" wrestlers step up to battle each other with only boxing gloves to protect themselves in "real" matches that lasted three rounds on *Monday Night Raw*. It was a disaster.

As a wrestling fan who has lived through the WWE's two boom periods in the mid '80s and late '90s, I have to admit that every time the lights dimmed in the arena for these bouts, simulating boxing matches or no-frills shoot fights, my stomach would knot up. I knew that what I was about to see, while unrehearsed, would be dull, slow and repetitive, and that the fans in the arena would join together in a chorus of boos. The TV audience would take this opportunity to flip over to *WCW Monday Nitro*. As any diehard WWE fan at the time could tell you, presenting real fights on *Raw* was a really bad idea. It was a difficult thing to watch the WWE do.

Brawl for All was initially designed to elevate veteran "Dr. Death" Steve Williams—considered by many behind the scenes to be one of the toughest men to lace wrestling boots in the '80s—to instant main-event status and boost his tough-guy mystique for a rock-hard series with the then red hot "Stone Cold" Steve Austin. But the Brawl ended up being won by the colorless former "Smokin' Gunn," Bart Gunn. The victory was a blow to Williams's career, and Gunn was subsequently fed to the wolves and hammered in 30 seconds in a worthless Brawl For All match against the boxer Butterbean at *WrestleMania XV.*

The WWF never tried the experiment again, in part, because of the severe injuries wrestlers incurred during these scuffles. (Williams was out for three months as a result of his participation, and the main-event plans for him were scrapped.) But more importantly, those running the company, no matter how much they tried, could not rig the ending. And because they couldn't rig who would win the Brawl, there was no way to guarantee that they would be able to take advantage of this series to promote those wrestlers who were good sports entertainers.

Fans hated the Brawl For All matches, often heckling them and then heading for the concession stands until the next match was lined up. After all, wrestling fans buy tickets because we want to cheer and boo and jeer and whistle for the characters we love and hate. It's our way of participating in their stories. We don't care whether wrestlers are really tough; we just want to believe that they are tough. We know it's a pre-arranged work. But that doesn't matter. We just want to be able to suspend disbelief for a few hours and scream our lungs out in a way that no other sport or spectacle will allow.

Wrestling fans will swallow reality only for so long. What they want is the larger-than-life battles that they pay to see, a fantasy that moves close to reality without going too far.

While Brawl For All may have left fans unimpressed, looking back at the long history of wrestling matches and how wrestlers and promoters took risks by walking on both sides of the line separating reality from fantasy, we see that what excites fans most is when they are given a healthy mixture of both. Wrestling certainly isn't real, and it never has been. But this certainly does not make it fake. The athletes behind the characters are quite real. So are the injuries they suffer, the career successes they experience and the emotions they generate in fans.

Wrestling's greatest matches are great not only for the stories told and the athleticism, creativity and spectacle on display between bells, but for the way in which these matches impact the lives of the men and women who compete in them, and how they've helped shape the business and art of pro wrestling.

MAT FACTS

George's Star

The '40s star Gorgeous George was one of wrestling's first true crossover superstars. Muhammad Ali and James Brown both acknowledge George's influence on their performance styles. George also appeared in the 1949 film, *Pardon My Toehold* (aka *Alias the Champ*). In 1951, Warner Brothers' Merry Melodies cartoon *Bunny Hugged* featured a character named Ravishing Ronald modeled after George.

Longest of the Long

Former 10-time AWA world champion Verne Gagne might be called the longest reigning world champion of all time. His 10 championships combine for a striking 4690 days as world titleholder. That bests runner up Bruno Sammartino by 650 days. But Bruno Sammartino's first reign as WWF champion remains the longest single world championship reign. It lasted from May 17, 1963, to January 18, 1971, an incredible 2803 days! Second longest is Verne Gagne's AWA title reign that ran from August 31, 1968 to November 8, 1975—2625 days. By contrast, the combined duration of "Stone Cold" Steve Austin's six WWF title reigns is a mere 529 days. Hulk Hogan's 14 world championships lasted 3369 days.

Shortest of the Short

On the flipside, 10 wrestlers have held world titles for less than a day. The shortest reigning world champion was Andre the Giant, who handed over the WWF title to "The Million Dollar Man" Ted DiBiase a mere 45 seconds after defeating Hulk Hogan on NBC's *The Main Event* on February 5, 1988. The second shortest reign goes to Yokozuna, who relinquished his WWF championship in an impromptu match with Hulk Hogan at *WrestleMania IX* just 2 minutes, 7 seconds after winning it.

Oldest of the Old

WWE chairman Vince McMahon became the oldest ever world champion when he lifted the ECW world title at the age of 61 years, 35 days. He's also the second oldest titleholder, having won the WWF title seven years earlier at the ripe old age of 54 years, 21 days.

Chapter Two

The Irresistible Force, The Immoveable Object

I don't believe it...I never thought it could be done, Gorilla!
                    –Jesse "The Body" Ventura

Could he do it? On March 29, 1987, over 93,000 fans from all corners of the United States, from all corners of Canada and even from overseas crammed into the Pontiac Silverdome outside Detroit, Michigan to find out. And they weren't disappointed. He could do it. That night—as wrestling fans young and old well remember—Hulk Hogan body-slammed the 525-pound, 7-foot 4-inch Andre the Giant.

Hogan was the last wrestler to leave the ring that night, leading his Hulkamaniacs and even his detractors, in one of the largest celebrations the sport of wrestling has ever produced. Afterwards, a cart wheeled him back down the aisle, his WWF title belt firmly in hand. Once behind the curtain he had crossed a half-hour before, the spotlight of the wrestling world left behind, Hogan leaned his forehead over into his folded arms in a symbol of prayer and relief. He had climbed to the top of the wrestling mountain.

But the ascent had not been easy, and Terry Bollea, the man everyone knew as Hulk Hogan, had been asking himself the same question the crowd had been asking in the long years leading up to this event: could he do it? In days and weeks prior to the match, he had doubted himself perhaps more than anyone else.

Bollea's first WWF stint from 1979 to 1981 had ended badly. Billed as "The Fabulous Hulk Hogan," Bollea was a heel managed by the cane-swinging "Classy" Freddie Blassie, who notoriously antagonized fans by calling them "pencil-necked geeks." After defeating the future "Million Dollar Man" Ted DiBiase at Madison Square Garden on December 17, 1979, Hogan's career prospects were looking up. Over the next two years he feuded with then World Wide Wrestling Federation champion Bob Backlund, former bodybuilder "Mr. U.S.A." Tony Atlas and, of course, a baby-faced behemoth named Andre the Giant.

The six-foot eight-inch tall, 300-pound Hogan was advertised as weighing a monstrous 330 pounds.

Like Andre, he was often pitted against two or three wrestlers at a time. Promoters saw in Hogan a competitor who could believably give Andre a run for his money.

Wrestlers often speak of climbing the "pecking order," of "paying their dues" to the industry and the veteran wrestlers at the top of the card. In the early 1980s, Andre made sure Hogan paid his dues. "There was some rough going between me and him," comments Hogan on their first series in 1980. "He'd get me in the ring and just tan my hide. I'd be on my way to the building to wrestle him, and I'd pull the car over and just vomit I was so scared and nervous. Every time I knew I had to wrestle him I just couldn't control myself."

"But then, after taking several beatings within an inch of my life," Hogan continues, "he gained respect for me."

Wrestling back then was very different from the sanitized world it is today. Says Hogan: "There's a lot of things that happened in this ring in the old days that wouldn't happen today. You think you're going to work and give a guy your arm and he tries to break it in half. There's a lot of things that've changed in this business that a lot of people just don't understand."

The young, boisterous, overconfident Hogan had one goal in mind at this point: to become just as big, just as impressive to the fans as Andre the Giant.

Hogan had to prove to fans that he could beat Andre, something he failed to accomplish in his first WWE stint. But he also had to show promoters that he deserved Andre's spot on the card and with it, more money and more opportunity in the spotlight. Hogan expressed his superiority to both spectators and WWWF officials alike. "And that was a direct threat to Andre," remarks Hogan.

But Andre proved to be an obstacle both in and out of the ring. Their feud in the ring, with Hogan as heel and Andre as babyface, culminated in a match on August 9, 1980, at New York's Shea Stadium two days before Hogan's 27th birthday. The card, titled The Showdown at Shea and headlined by a steel cage match between Bruno Sammartino and his turncoat apprentice Larry Zbysko, was attended by a pumped crowd of 38,295. On this occasion, Hogan battled Andre valiantly, but when the referee accidentally became incapacitated, Andre took control of the bout. He executed a bone-crushing 500-pound splash onto a prone Hogan and a substitute referee slapped the mat three times. The referee called for the match-ending bell a split-second before Hogan could kick out.

Hogan and manager Blassie were not satisfied with the outcome. As the crowd rejoiced and Andre raised his arms in victory, a frustrated Hogan stuffed his elbow pad with a metal plate, fired Andre into the ropes and caught the fan favorite from Grenoble, France, with a blow that left a gash on Andre's fore-head. Struggling to his feet and bearing what the dean of wrestling announcers, Gordon Solie, famously dubbed "the crimson mask," a dazed Andre was nevertheless announced as the winner. A dejected Hogan was booed out of Shea Stadium, his bid to unseat Andre and take his spot in the wrestling world overturned.

Not long thereafter, at the end of 1980, Terry Bollea started to hear rumors that Hollywood icon Sylvester Stallone wanted him to play a role in his upcoming film, *Rocky III* (1982). Bollea couldn't believe it at first, dismissing the gossip as a prank. But when he received a telephone call from Stallone himself offering him the role, Bollea was ecstatic, believing that this would be the break he needed to lift his career to new heights.

Unfortunately, Vince McMahon, Sr., the promoter to whom Hogan owed his recent WWWF successes, didn't see it that way. "Terry, you're a wrestler, not a movie star. You're booked in Greensboro tomorrow to wrestle for Jim Crockett Promotions," Vince, Sr. insisted. "Well, Mr. McMahon, I told you I was going to work for Mr. Stallone for 10 days to do this movie," Hogan replied. McMahon was a tradition-alist and didn't see how he could use Hogan's Hollywood stint to enhance his wrestling box office potential. Both McMahon and Hogan held their ground until McMahon gave Hogan an ultimatum: "Terry, if you go act and don't go wrestle where I tell you to, then you'll never work here again." Despite such a weighted threat from such a powerful promoter, Hogan took his chances and made his silver screen debut as the seven foot, 350-pound "Thunderlips, the Ultimate Male" in the Stallone-directed box office hit. He never expected to wrestle for the WWWF again. His dream of becoming bigger than Andre was, for moment at least, dashed.

Meanwhile, Andre's ring career flourished in a bitter feud with the Mongolian terror, Killer Khan, accompanied by Hogan's former manager, Fred Blassie. In a match held in Rochester, New York, Khan maliciously snapped Andre's ankle with a well-placed knee-drop. Fans gasped. Never had Andre seemed so vulnerable. In actuality, this storyline injury concealed a legitimate injury Andre suffered while getting out of bed one morning in the fall of 1981. Sensing that a public announcement revealing that the mighty Andre the Giant had broken his ankle in such a careless way would do little for Andre or his feud with Khan, promoters decided to write Andre's injury into the long-term program. Fans therefore awaited Andre's return with anticipation, looking forward to the day that he'd exact revenge on the evil Mongolian. A determined Andre settled the score with Khan on November 14, 1981, at the Philadelphia Spectrum, destroying his opponent in a Mongolian Stretcher Match. As the battered Khan was wheeled to the dressing room on a stretcher, the fans roared. Andre's star had never shined so bright.

In the wake of his *Rocky III* role, Hogan found bookings with the Minneapolis-based AWA, where he would compete for the next three years. Initially pushed as a heel and managed by "Luscious" Johnny Valiant, Hogan eventually turned babyface for the first time in his career. AWA fans simply wouldn't boo Hogan, who now strutted to the ring to the sounds of the Oscar-nominated *Rocky* theme song, *The Eye of the Tiger.* Hogan's brush with Hollywood had given him the larger-than-life aura of a star. The seeds of Hulkamania were planted.

"It wasn't as big as it became," states Hogan in 2002, reflecting back on those early days of Hulkamania, "but it was starting to bubble, to come up from the ground."

At this stage in the evolution of the industry, wrestlers marketed their own characters. Hogan recalls going to local malls to print up t-shirts bearing catchphrases he developed himself: "Hulkamania Running Wild" and, in reference to his accumulated battle scars, "One Scar, One Million Enemies." His fans gobbled these shirts up at concession stands.

In the AWA, Hogan honed his in-ring skills, developed his trademark interview style and polished crucial aspects of the Hulk Hogan character that would only a few years later capture the hearts of millions. He also met longtime friend and legendary wrestling interviewer, "Mean" Gene Okerlund. "The first time the t-shirt was torn off," reminisces former AWA star and promoter, Greg Gagne, "we were in Chicago, at the Rosemont Horizon. The atmosphere was just electric when Hogan, Jim Brunzell and I entered the ring. Hulk just stood there in his pose, and Jim and I grabbed one side of the t-shirt and tore it off of him real slow. And the people just blow the roof right off that place. After that, when he came out, he just tore off the t-shirt."

In short order, Verne Gagne (the father of Greg Gagne) pushed Hogan to main event status. Gagne held notoriously conservative views about the sport of wrestling and played down the entertainment side of the industry, but he was forced to listen to the fans: they wanted to see their man Hogan, a big blond, charismatic power wrestler who relied on high-impact blows rather than traditional wrestling takedowns and technique. They wanted to see him in main events and were excited at the prospect of him winning the AWA world title. But it was not to be.

In his April 1982 feud with titleholder Nick Bockwinkel, Hogan pinned the champion, but fell victim to shoddy officiating. Hogan's title-winning three-count was overturned as a result of the use of a foreign object, and the title remained around the Bockwinkel's waist.

Behind the scenes, Terry Bollea's frustration with AWA booking was building. He could not understand why Gagne refused to ride the wave of Hogan's newfound popularity and grant him a run as world champion. A determined Hulk had a new t-shirt printed that read, "We Want The Belt!"

Fans enthusiastically chanted this phrase throughout Hogan's heated match against Bockwinkel on April 23, 1983. Executing his trademark legdrop on Bockwinkel, the referee counted three. Fans leapt out of their chairs in celebration. Hogan had finally climbed to the top of the ladder! "Hulk Hogan has done it! Hulk Hogan is the champion! He's got the belt!" exclaimed the play-by-play commentator, as Hogan paraded around the ring displaying the AWA title belt. Moments later, "Mean" Gene made the fateful announcement: "Ladies and gentlemen, I have just been informed that AWA president Stanley Blackburn is of the opinion that Hulk Hogan threw Nick Bockwinkel over the top rope. Because of that, the Hulk is disqualified, and the belt remains with Nick Bockwinkel." Hogan's victory was annulled.

Cheated, the fans met the decision with a chorus of boos and eventually came together in an ear-ringing chant of "B******t!" Some felt so swindled that they began to toss debris into the ring. Hogan clearly sympathized with their response, grabbing the AWA championship belt and flinging it to the mat in the ultimate act of disrespect. He had failed to reach the upper echelon of the industry once again.

The WWF's new owner, Vince McMahon, Jr., would remedy the AWA's blunder. Reneging on his father's threat and seeing Hogan's potential, he called Terry Bollea in late 1983, inviting him back to the Northeast. Bollea accepted. Hanging up the phone, Bollea, somewhat cynical that any promoter would stand by him for an extended period, immediately turned to his wife: "If we have one good year in New York, then we can retire forever."

His years of struggle in the industry had finally paid off.

A few short weeks later in January 1984, Hogan pinned the Iron Sheik at Madison Square Garden, winning the WWF title. Announcer Gorilla Monsoon cried "Hulkamania is here!" and the WWF blasted off into national and international dominance of the wrestling industry.

In his post-match interview after defeating the Iron Sheik, Hogan caught up with an old friend.

"It is like the dream of a lifetime, daddy," he confessed to Mean Gene, "It's like going to the mountaintop a thousand times over!" Walking in to interrupt the interview, Andre the Giant poured a bottle of champagne over the Hulkster, congratulating him on his win. "I am really proud of you," stated Andre in his deep voice, shaking Hogan's hand. Once again, reality seeped into the scene: "Thank you, Boss," relied Hogan, calling Andre by his off-screen nickname.

With Hulkamania running wild, the WWF's new owner, Vince McMahon, Jr., acquired all the best talent from around the country and, breaking unwritten rules and crossing imaginary boundaries separating the country's regional promotions, booked his talent to wrestle on cards all over the U.S. Hogan defended the title against the likes of "Rowdy" Roddy Piper on MTV's *The War to Settle the Score* and the 450-pound, "Walking Condominium" King Kong Bundy at *WrestleMania II* in Los Angeles. With each of these victories, the popularity of the WWF and Hulkamania reached new heights. But, Hogan soon realized that to prove his dominance, he'd have to defend his title against an old foe: Andre the Giant.

"When I came back in '83," recollects Hogan, "I didn't go head-to-head with Andre at first. About '84–'85, there were rumblings that Andre and I should wrestle. *WrestleMania III*, I really had to prove myself to Andre. That was the ultimate test."

The only obstacle in the way for promoter Vince McMahon was that, with *WrestleMania III* just around the corner, Andre was on leave from wrestling, in semi-retirement due to a severe back injury. "As much as Andre meant to my dad, which is everything," Vince, Jr., remembers, "I called Andre and said I want to ask you something." "If it's about the business," replied Andre, "then save your airfare." "Just hear me out," Vince retorted. "Vince," Andre explained, "my back, I need an operation—I'm done." McMahon knew how important this match was for Hogan and how much of a draw and a spectacle this event would be. McMahon managed to convince Andre to return.

The storyline was launched in early 1987. Onscreen, Hogan and Andre were close friends, almost brothers, often teaming up to rid the ring of rule-breaking vermin. But one thing irked Andre so much that he would turn heel.

It all started when Hogan was presented a large trophy commemorating the third anniversary of his title reign by onscreen WWF president Jack Tunney. Not long after, on *Piper's Pit*, Andre was honored with a substantially smaller trophy, commemorating his being undefeated for 15 years.

The Hulkster came out to congratulate his friend and mentor. "Andre the Giant is number one," shouted Hogan on this day. "I'd like to thank you for recognizing in my book the real champion of superstars all over the world." As Hogan spoke, Andre glared over at his puny trophy. Moments later, he marched off the stage, insulted.

On a subsequent edition of *Piper's Pit*, Andre, now flanked by his new manager, Bobby "The Brain" Heenan, confronted Hogan. Pointing his finger in Hogan's face, Andre made his intentions clear: "Look at me when I am talking to you. I am here for one reason: to challenge you for a world championship match at *Wrestlemania*." "Andre, please, no, it's not happening," a perplexed Hogan pleaded. "We're friends, Andre, PLEASE!" An arrogant Heenan interjected: "You don't believe it? Maybe you'll believe this, Hogan!" Andre proceeded to tear off Hogan's shirt and, with it, the trademark crucifix the Hulkster carried around his neck. Piper was determined to get an answer. "Yes or no, are you or are you not going to fight him at *WrestleMania III* for the world heavyweight championship?" Mulling it over, Hogan replied emphatically: "YESSS!!"

Promoters were concerned about Andre on match day. Having just undergone back surgery and ballooned to a whopping 525 pounds due to inactivity, Andre's bones and joints were in a great deal of pain. It was not certain whether he'd be able to compete. In order to wrestle, he would have to wear a large brace compressing his back and ribs for support under his singlet.

Hogan had another good reason to worry in the hours leading up to the March 29 match, even if he was at the top of the wrestling mountain.

Rumors reached Hogan that Andre might not "put him over" in their match, backstage talk for allowing oneself to be pinned. Vince McMahon himself approached Hogan early in the day, warning him not to purposefully or accidentally disrespect Andre that night, or else Andre would refuse to allow Hogan to win the match. Finally, so close to achieving what he had always dreamed, Bollea couldn't misstep now.

Stepping out from behind the curtain, greeted by nearly 100,000 spectators live in attendance and millions more on pay-per-view and closed circuit television, Hogan walked the aisle. As special guest ring announcer, baseball legend Bob Uecker, introduced Hogan, and the fans erupted. Hogan walked slowly into the ring and stared eye-to-eye with his seven-foot opponent, slowly tearing his t-shirt from his torso. *Entertainment Tonight* co-host Mary Hart rang the bell, and the most anticipated match of the '80s was underway.

"Look at the stare on the champion," commented play-by-play announcer Gorilla Monsoon.

"The irresistible force meeting the immoveable object."

Perhaps overanxious, Hogan "Hulked up" early, unloading at the beginning with a series of right hands to Andre's head and hastily scooping Andre in an attempted body slam. To no avail. Hogan fell backwards toward the mat, Andre's entire weight crashing down on top of him. "Was that two, or was that three?" inquired color commentator Jesse "The Body" Ventura. Amazingly, Andre earned a long two-count, nearly pinning Hogan in record time. Hogan was severely hurt.

A confident Andre dominated the next several minutes of the bout, unloading with heavy-handed chops, forearm blows and bodyslams, even at one point walking over the back of a prone Hulkster. "You know, it almost seems at this point in the bout that it's a mismatch," spurted a stunned Ventura. The action was slow, but the fans watched every move intently.

Hogan attempted a comeback, rocking the Giant with fisticuffs and an elbow smash, but Andre soon regained control, trapping Hogan in the world's biggest bear hug. Hogan survived Andre's air-sapping squeeze, and several minutes later, the action spilled out onto the arena floor. Andre cornered Hogan and attempted a headbutt. This time, Hogan ducked and Andre's massive skull struck the iron ring post. Desperate, Hogan attempted a foolhardy piledriver on the concrete floor. Andre's massive girth proved too much for Hogan.

Back in the ring, Andre seemed to be firmly in control. But the Hulkster's mobility helped him avoid a big boot. Coming off the ropes, Hogan connected with a massive clothesline, downing the French behemoth. The Pontiac Silverdome exploded! Heenan rushed over to console the fallen giant. "That's the first time I think the Giant's ever been knocked off his feet like that," Ventura exclaimed.

Hogan's time had arrived. "He's 'Hulking up,' Jess," remarked Monsoon. Coming to his feet, shaking with adrenaline and feeding off the electrified crowd, he turned to the fans and nodded, "Yes," as if to signal that this was the moment. Monsoon: "We're seeing what this guy is really made of, why he is the greatest professional athlete in the world today!" Hogan staggered over Andre and crotched him. "Look at this!" shouted Monsoon. Hogan lifted Andre up into the air and twisted his body into the launch position. Andre let out a loud groan, his feet flailing about. Finally, his huge frame hit the mat with a massive thud. "He slammed him," screamed Ventura, "I don't believe it!" As 93,000 fans erupted, the Hulkster hit the ropes and connected with his flying leg-drop, earning the pinfall.

"I never thought it could be done, Gorilla," confessed Jesse Ventura.

Hogan had finally fulfilled his dream. On one of the greatest stages wrestling history has ever known, in an event that marked the pinnacle of wrestling's golden age, Hulk Hogan had bodyslammed and pinned the legendary Andre the Giant. It was the crowning achievement of a nearly decade-long journey to the top.

Vince McMahon later commented on the importance of this event: "I was so proud of Andre on that day, and proud of Hogan. I wouldn't say that it was a passing of the torch as much as it was a 'good housekeeping' seal of approval. Now Hulk had Andre's stamp. It doesn't get any bigger than that."

MAT FACTS

"Never Been Slammed" Myth

Over the course of their *WrestleMania III* clash, announcers Gorilla Monsoon and Jesse Ventura both claimed that Andre had never been slammed. In fact, Hogan slammed Andre during their August 9, 1980, bout at Shea Stadium.

"Never Been Beaten in 15 Years" Myth

In the lead up to *WrestleMania III,* the WWF also wanted fans to believe that Andre hadn't been beaten in 15 years in order to make the challenge presented seem even more insurmountable for the Hulkster. However, Andre the Giant, born Andre Roussimoff, actually had lost cleanly in non-WWF matches even in the '80s. He suffered a pinfall loss in Mexico to El Canek in 1984. In Japan, he suffered a submission loss to Antonio Inoki in 1986. He also lost in a controversial no-contest finish against Akira Maeda, who broke with the storyline and used shoot-style tactics to neutralize Andre's size advantage. Amazingly, the massive man also contested 60-minute time limit draws with the two other major world champions of the day, Harley Race and Nick Bockwinkel.

His First World Title?

The WWF title that Hogan won on January 24, 1984, was not his first. On June 2, 1983, Hogan defeated Antonio Inoki to crown the first ever IWGP world champion, the signature title of what would become the New Japan Pro Wrestling (or NJPW) promotion. Also, the AWA, revived in 1996, retroactively recognized his two AWA title wins over Nick Bockwinkel in 1982–83. With his six WWF/WWE title reigns and six WCW title reigns, this makes Hogan a 15-time world champion.

What's In A Name?

Terry Bollea went through several monikers before settling on "Hulk Hogan," including "Terry Boulder" and "Sterling Golden." Andre at various points in his career went as "Butcher Roussimoff," "Giant Roussimoff," "Monster Roussimoff," "Eiffel Tower," "Monster Eiffel Tower," "Jean Ferré," and "Géant Ferré."

A Giant Disorder

Throughout most of his career, promoters tried to take advantage of Andre's impressive frame by announcing him at a variety of weights and heights. He was billed early in his career as being seven-feet tall. This was exaggerated in the early 1970s to 7'4" and sometimes to 7'5" with a weight that ranged from 309 pounds to 550 pounds. His actual height is contested, and there has been much speculation and debate over the issue. Jim Duggan and manager Bobby Heenan maintain that his WWF-billed height of 7'4" was correct. Wrestling journalist Dave Meltzer wrote in his book *Tributes* that Chuck Wepner, who faced Andre in a boxer vs. wrestler match in 1976, told reporters Andre was 6'10". Wepner's manager said Andre made the 6'5" tall Wepner look like a baby beside Andre. In Meltzer's second book, *Tributes II,* Meltzer claims Andre was measured at 6' 9¾" 1974 by a French athletic commission at age 28. Meltzer also estimated Andre at 6'11" when comparing him to fellow *Conan the Destroyer* star Wilt Chamberlain in 1984. However, Mike Mooneyham, another wrestling journalist, maintained in his obituary of Andre in 1994 that Andre was 7'2" when he began wrestling. The exaggeration of his height probably comes from the fact that Kareem Abdul-Jabbar was the tallest renowned athlete in the world at the time at 7'2", and promoters wanted to bill Roussimoff as the biggest athlete in the world. Nevertheless, the sight of him alone was enough to draw huge crowds during a time when there were only a handful of wrestlers over 6'6". His condition, which included symptoms such as enlarged hands and feet and exaggerated facial features, likely aided the visual perception of him appearing larger than he actually was. Back surgeries and posture problems later in life also contributed to his decrease in height.

Height Advantage

Andre was not the tallest wrestler ever. Standing at a legitimate 7'6" tall, Giant Gonzalez, who wrestled for the WWF in 1993 and in WCW before that as "El Gigante," holds the record.

Current *Smackdown!* star The Great Khali stands at 7'3". The Big Show is billed as being seven feet tall. Beyond these goliaths of the squared circle, legend has it that a '50s wrestler by the name of Paul Bunyan, born Max Palmer, stood 8'2" tall, but this height measurement was almost certainly exaggerated.

Chapter Three

The Rivalry

We'd do what the name on the marquee says, we'd wrestle.

–Ric Flair

Some fans simply refer to the Ricky Steamboat vs. Ric Flair feud as "the Rivalry." And for much of the '80s and '90s, it was and a memorable one at that. Rumors have been flying for years that the WWE wants to pit these gladiators against one another for one last match at an upcoming *WrestleMania*. But it has yet to happen.

While this nostalgic rematch would be special for longtime wrestling fans, it is doubtful that Flair and Steamboat—both far past their primes—would be able to muster the heat and pure athleticism on display in their classic back-and-forth contests over the NWA world title in the late '80s. Wrestling purists have long lauded these bouts as the pinnacle of North American wrestling craftsmanship and technique.

"I would say that I have probably wrestled Steamboat 3000 times in my career," Ric Flair reminisces. "I wrestled him every other night for about five years. He's the best I was ever in the ring with." Coming from perhaps the greatest wrestler of all time, these comments are not to be taken lightly.

There is and will forever remain a mutual respect amongst Flair and Steamboat. "I think that Rick has a huge respect for me. I know that I have it for him," confesses Flair. As any pro wrestler knows, mutual respect is a key ingredient in the relationship between any two wrestlers who want to assemble for the fans the quality matches for which Flair and Steamboat are known.

Former six-time AWA world titleholder Nick Bockwinkel once explained how mutual respect drives wrestlers to compete even harder in the ring. "It's a little psychological thing between the two guys getting in the ring. A little one-upmanship. The move you made, I made and a little bit better. There's that competitive thing there. Once that bell rings, you better be idling at 4000 rpms."

There's no better way to express what was going through the minds of Flair and Steamboat in their classic three-match feud in 1989. "We both excelled athletically," Flairs explains. "We both were in tremendous shape. And we pushed each other. I refused to take a deep breath, and he was the same way. We just went at each other wide-open, 120 percent for 60 minutes. We thrived on the idea that we were the best at what we did. We wanted to prove it."

Trust, desire and athleticism pushed Flair and Steamboat to wrestle at a level that few could match. And fans loved it. Their bouts were intense, non-stop marathons. Each man knew the other's move before they could execute it. "When we'd wrestle, we'd only get going at 15–20 minutes," says Flair with pride. "We'd do what the name on the marquee says, we'd wrestle. Hold-for-hold. It was easy with him."

Steamboat agrees: "We liked to work, and we knew we could. We felt so comfortable with each other."

These contests also serve as a useful reminder of how unscripted a wrestling contest can be when the combatants are skilled and have learned to trust each other. Commenting on the famous pair's best two-of-three falls, 60-minute blinder at NWA's *Clash of the Champions VI* on April 2, 1989, Steamboat casually states: "The only thing we had was the finish. The rest, we just winged it, and called it in the ring."

The contrast between this series and the WWF's storylines at the time is telling. Yes, "Macho Man" Randy Savage's heated 18-minute title defense against Hulk Hogan at *WrestleMania V* stands as one the best matches of the year. But in general, the WWF's matches tended to be shorter and demanded less conditioned and skilled performers. The WWF's roster consisted mainly of 280- to 300-pound lumbering brawlers who rarely fought for more 10 to 12 minutes. Worse, the smaller, better-conditioned, more technically skilled stars in the WWF were encouraged to tone down their moves and to conform to the balance of the WWF's in-ring action. When Hulk Hogan defended the WWF title against the cartoonish Honky Tonk Man in an overbooked, interference-laden *Saturday Night's Main Event* romp the same summer that saw Flair and Steamboat setting fire to NWA rings with 30- to 60-minute scorchers, the match lasted a mere 6 minutes and 15 seconds.

Clearly, athleticism was taking a back seat to caricature and low-impact antics between bells in the WWF. And the fans knew it. They also know that the NWA wrestling network was the place to go for genuine pro wrestling competition.

Of the three high-profile televised bouts between Flair and Steamboat in 1989, the *WrestleWar '89* match on May 7 stands out. It would be the capstone match at this stage of their remarkable rivalry. In fact, though their April 2 contest and their 23-minute *Chi-Town Rumble* belter on February 20 are both memorable, the May 7 *WrestleWar* bout is often cited as one of the greatest wrestling matches of all time.

Set for one fall with a 60-minute time limit, Flair-Steamboat III would have a special stipulation added that spoke volumes about the caliber of these athletes. Aware that Flair and Steamboat were evenly matched and could easily wrestle the time limit without either man scoring a decision, NWA officials decided that, in the event of draw, a decision would be rendered by a group of judges specially selected for the event. They would sit at ringside and hand in scorecards to the NWA announce crew at 15-minute intervals. The judges were three former NWA world champions: Terry Funk, Pat O'Connor and Lou Thesz. No one else was better suited for the job.

This stipulation not only lent the contest the aura of a legitimate wrestling match, but added to the excitement experienced by fans sitting at home. Every 15 minutes, they would see how the judges were scoring the wrestlers' performances. Fans could also be certain that this match would have a clear-cut winner.

All the ingredients were in place for a compelling, no-nonsense championship bout.

As they were announced by ring announcer Gary Michael Cappetta at a lean 242 and 237 pounds respectively, former five-time champ Flair and the defending titleholder Steamboat paced in their corners, pausing only to get in some last minute stretching. "Many say that this is Flair's last chance," explained play-by-play man Jim Ross, also warming up. The crowd of 5200 at the Nashville Municipal Auditorium cheered for both men during the introductions out of respect and then took their seats in anticipation.

After the opening bell, Flair and Steamboat felt each other out with a rudimentary collar-and-elbow tie-up, followed by a clean break in the ropes. After another collar-and-elbow, Steamboat caught the Nature Boy slightly off-guard with a lightning-quick armdrag takeover. Both wrestlers were somewhat cautious at this stage.

Coming off the ropes, Flair took Steamboat down with a shoulder block. Steamboat fired back with high hip-lock takeover and a classic Steamboat-style, deep armdrag. Steamboat then neutralized Flair with an armlock. Frustrated, Flair backed his foe into a corner and paintbrushed him with a series of insulting slaps to the head. Steamboat, showing no intimidation, went tit-for-tat with Flair, slapping "Slic" Ric to the canvas. There was no love lost here, but these determined competitors had yet to put the key in the ignition.

"It should be an offensive match, indeed, with the judging system as it is," stated Ross, in a spot-on analysis. As fans would soon find out, neither man would show any restraint. Being on the defensive meant being on the short end of the points tally. For Flair and Steamboat, the pressure to outdo one another had never been so intense.

Turning the tide, Flair backed Steamboat into a corner and unloaded with a forearm blow to the midsection and a shotgun-like chop to the chest. The sound of flesh meeting flesh resonated throughout the hall. As the fans celebrated the action with a familiar "Whooo!" Flair connected with another chop. "Man, that just sends chills up your spine," winced Ross.

Not to be outdone, the Dragon retaliated with a thunderous knife-edge of his own. The chop-fest was on! Both men exchanged a series of smacks to the chest that would leave any normal man doubled over, eyes watering and clutching his torso. Flair chopped Steamboat. Steamboat chopped Flair. Chop! Chop! Chop! Spinning about, the Hawaii native sent Flair staggering back with the mother of all chops. The Dragon then connected with three unanswered chops of his own. "This is indeed the NWA!" announced Ross proudly, emphasizing the physicality of the contest.

After being elevated with a back-bodydrop, Flair scooted off the floor for a breather. "Neither man is giving an edge," stated Ross. But Flair had been bested in this early exchange.

Returning to the ring, Flair managed to slow the pace with a side-headlock. Steamboat, anticipating Flair's every move precisely, countered with an overhand wristlock, engaging Flair in a test of strength. Powering Flair to the canvas, thus proving himself the stronger man, Steamboat hooked in an arm bar and went to work on Flair's left appendage. Trying to resist, Flair came to his feet, only to be grounded again with another deep armdrag.

Evaluating the move closely, Ross estimated: "I don't think anybody executes an armdrag any better than The Dragon."

These men were engaged in a careful game of chess, with Steamboat momentarily on the offensive.

Wrestling fans noticed in these early stages of the bout that Steamboat was executing a carefully thought-out game plan: to work on Flair's arm. He did just that with pinpoint precision for the next several minutes, with hammerlocks and a series of well-placed knee- and elbow-drops. The Dragon had had success before with this strategy, making Flair submit to an excruciating double-chicken wing armlock in the second fall of their April 2 match-up. Would he have repeat success with this plan of attack?

Out of desperation, Flair responded with another series of crowd-rousing chops and even a hair pull but failed to break Steamboat's spirit. Perhaps finally sensing a momentum change, Flair blasted Steamboat with a round of heavy-handed forearm blows and then peppered his reeling opponent with a few more chops.

But these chops only served to re-ignite the Dragon's flame! He overwhelmed the Charlotte, North Carolina native with another series of flesh-burning knife-edges. Wrestling has perhaps never known two greater chop-masters! Then he went right back to work on Flair's damaged wing.

Ten minutes into the contest, the pace quickened, but only for a moment. Steamboat dropkicked Flair over the top rope and outside the ring. Flair was in trouble, and he knew it.

Steamboat was at the top of his game. He had until this point foiled every one of Flair's attempts to gain control of the bout. With the first set of judges' scores imminent, Flair had to come up with something.

Quickening the pace once again in an attempt to find a hole in his opponent's game plan, Flair landed a perfectly executed high hiplock takeover sending The Dragon crashing to the mat. "Never sell this man short!" remarked color commentator Bob Caudle. Flair had found his opening. But was it too late to score points with the ringside judges?

As the Nature Boy unloaded with a series of chops to Steamboat's defenseless torso, Jim Ross announced what Flair himself knew at this point: the judges decided unanimously to award the first quarter-hour to Steamboat. His arm aching, his chest beet-red from The Dragon's lethal chops, and slightly demoralized by having to play a game of catch up behind his focused foe, Flair needed to reverse his fortunes.

"He's been in so many important matches, he's gotta know that the tide is so far favoring Steamboat and that he's got to turn it loose," commented Caudle. Steamboat had snuffed out every attempt by Flair to get the upper hand.

Flair and Steamboat read the crowd responses carefully, awaiting just the right moment to stage a Flair comeback. This is just how they had wrestled their *Clash of the Champions* contest. Steamboat remembered that best-of-three-falls war well. Prior to the match, another wrestler asked him how much of the match he and Flair had worked out aside from the falls. Steamboat replied, "Hell, we're just gonna call it in the ring."

"We would see how the crowd was going and take it from there," continues Steamboat. "We knew each other so well that sometimes, without talking, we'd go into a spot we both remembered from 10 years earlier."

Not many wrestlers handled matches like this. Both Steamboat and Flair had had difficulties during their respective feuds with Randy Savage. Unlike Flair and Steamboat, Savage tended to practice his matches and script every hold to the second. "Make no mistake about it," Flair adds, "I respect Randy Savage for his skills and accomplishments. But because of his unwillingness to just get in the ring and improvise, I won't call him a great worker." Improvisation, careful crowd reading—this is just what Flair and Steamboat were doing during their *WrestleWar* contest.

As the bout rolled on, Steamboat continued to trip-up Flair. Flair might connect with a shoulder block or a chop or two, but Steamboat never allowed him to string together a series of high-impact moves. If he felt the momentum shifting, he'd dig down deep and lash out with blows of his own. The Dragon was stoic and focused at this stage, never even pausing to address the raucous Nashville crowd. He was "in the zone," wrestling a determined and low-risk contest.

Perched on the second turnbuckle, The Dragon rattled the Nature Boy's brains with 10 well-placed karate chops to the forehead. He fired Flair into the opposite corner so hard that Flair flipped over into the turnbuckles like a rag doll. How, if at all, would the former five-time champ turn things around?

Even a competitor as concentrated as Steamboat eventually makes a mistake. Fortunately for Flair, it was a costly one.

Running off the ropes with too much momentum, looking to finish Flair off, Steamboat was sent sailing over the top rope and crashing to the arena floor. This was the break Flair was looking for.

It is in situations like this that champions define themselves. Despite being on the receiving end of punishment for the first 17 minutes of the bout, and having seen his every move and hold easily solved by The Dragon, Flair did not lose his composure. Maintaining his calm, he was now ready to dish out his own punishment. In this clash of wrestling titans, Steamboat's mettle would now be put to the test.

Flair blasted Steamboat with a chop so hard that the champ tumbled over the guardrail into the crowd and onto the concrete floor. These men were truly putting their bodies on the line for what was at the time the most respected prize in the wrestling world.

After connecting with a solid elbow to Steamboat's throat, Flair climbed back into the ring. The ringside fans shouted encouragement to their soft-spoken hero. "Get back in the ring, Ricky!" screamed one fan. "Don't let up!"

He didn't.

As Flair climbed from the ring and approached him to deliver another vicious chop, The Dragon dug down once again and met Flair with a chop of his own. The fans exploded with excitement. These men were truly laying the leather! Stunned at Steamboat's resilience, Flair turned and sprinted away from his incensed foe, climbing over cameramen and reporters at ringside as he circled the ring. The Dragon was in hot pursuit.

Sliding under the bottom rope, Flair came to his feet, believing he had shaken the champ. But Steamboat came off the top rope with a scintillating flying karate chop to the top of Flair's cranium. The crowd popped! Knocked silly, Flair spun around and flopped face-first to the mat. Not one person in attendance was seated.

"Just when the match looked like it had moved to the corner of the challenger, 'Nature Boy' Ric Flair, it looks like it's moved again!" exclaimed Caudle. The crowd was buzzing.

Steamboat, relentless in his attack on Flair's arm, returned to an armlock. The master of the figure four leglock had seen his attempt to change the tide of the bout backfire on him!

Attempting a high cross-body block, Steamboat once again found himself on the arena floor. Could Flair maintain the momentum this time?

Flair's bid for his sixth world championship took a turn for the better as the Nature Boy connected with two of his patented rolling knee-drops, several more physical chops to Steamboat's sternum and a variety of suplexes. These led to a number of near-falls. In a couple instances Flair was less than half a count away from being crowned champion. Frustrated with the cadence of the referee's count, Flair lashed out at the referee: "Hey! You'd better learn how to count or you'll be working somewhere else tomorrow!"

Upping the ante, Flair suplexed the hapless Dragon on the arena floor.

The second round of judge's scores came in early. Two of three judges gave Flair the edge. But the champion remained ahead on points in the total tally. Flair had to keep the pressure on!

As he attempted to suplex Steamboat into the ring from the apron, Steamboat flipped Flair over, avoiding the move, and rolled Flair up in a pinning combination. One… Two… Flair kicked out just before the three!

The action now was non-stop, and the audience was riled up to a fever pitch! Steamboat fired Flair into the ropes, and Flair came off with a flying cross-body of his own. Steamboat caught him, but the momentum sent both men soaring over the top strand. They both smacked the floor and lay motionless at ringside.

"Both men could be seriously hurt, here—that was a long fall out of that ring," spurted a concerned Caudle. The referee exercised his 10-count.

Coming to his feet first, Flair threw The Dragon into the ring. He needed to put Steamboat away and decided to climb to the top rope. The champ rose suddenly to his feet, crotched his defenseless opponent and tossed Flair off the top rope to the canvas in a king-sized bodyslam.

Steamboat was charged, pumping his arms as the adrenaline flowed throughout his battle-scarred body. He unloaded with several chops and a back-drop, eventually cradling Flair for another near-fall. Steamboat decided to go for broke. He perched Flair on the top turnbuckle and executed a thunderous superplex. This was the set up. As Flair writhed in pain, Steamboat came up from behind and hooked him in his dreaded double chicken-wing. Would Flair submit for the second time in his career?

Luckily, Flair was close to the ropes and was able to grab hold of them. The referee broke the hold. Undaunted, Steamboat climbed to the top rope. In one of the most spectacular spots in the match, Flair, seemingly out on his feet, stumbled over to the ropes as The Dragon was set to pounce and rocked the ropes just enough to make Steamboat lose his balance and fall 15 feet to the arena floor!

Outside, Steamboat clutched his knee. The master of the figure four smelled blood.

Suplexing Steamboat back into the ring, Flair went right to work on the knee, connecting with crushing blows and pulling and wrenching the joint in every direction he could. For Flair, the title was in sight! A submission victory seemed just around the corner.

On his first attempt, Flair grapevined Steamboat's leg and hooked in the figure four. The crowd rose to its feet. Would Steamboat submit?

As the match crossed the 30-minute mark, Steamboat was in the fight of his life, trying to endure Flair's excruciating submission hold.

"I want to tell you something, Bob, when fans tune in for a championship match, and they hear that 30 minutes have gone by, they know it's the NWA!" Ross stated, taking a jab at the WWF. "Wrestlers are not out here posing to rock 'n' roll music. These are great athletes competing for the richest prize in this sport, and they are puttin' it all on the line!"

Steamboat reached the ropes. Flair's assault on the champ's leg continued. He connected with a series of heavy blows to the knee. The Dragon's leg was virtually useless. But he didn't stop fighting. After countering Flair with a well-placed *insiguri* head kick, Steamboat attempted to body slam the challenger. His knee buckled. As Flair rolled through with the move, he wrapped Steamboat up in a small package. One... Two... THREE!

At 31:37, an overwhelmed Steamboat was counted down! And we had a new world heavy-weight champion!

Going hold-for-hold for just over half an hour, Steamboat and Flair assembled one of wrestling history's greatest, most physical pure wrestling contests.

Gasping for oxygen, Flair had his hand raised, and he collected his prize. He had won his sixth of 16 world championships, tying Lou Thesz's record.

A defeated Steamboat, who had brought a great deal of class and professionalism to the championship during his two-and-a-half-month title reign, walked up to his arch-rival and extended his hand. These two gladiators shook hands in a symbol of mutual admiration and sportsmanship.

Announcer Jim Ross joined Flair in the ring. "Ladies and gentlemen, we have seen history in the making," stated Ross, addressing the audience. "Ricky 'The Dragon' Steamboat and Ric Flair just competed in one of the greatest matches that any of us have ever witnessed." The Nashville crowd joined Ross in celebrating these men with applause.

They had indeed witnessed history.

Flair, stepping out of his "wheelin,' dealin,' kiss-stealin'" character, complemented his opponent in front of the appreciative crowd. "Rick Steamboat is the greatest champion I have ever faced."

MAT FACTS

"I Quit!"

Steamboat became the first wrestler to make Flair submit when he won the second fall of their *Clash of the Champions VI* battle.

You Never Know

Steamboat did not know he was set to defeat Flair for the NWA world title until the day he actually wrested it from the Nature Boy. Comments Steamboat: "When we got to the building, neither Flair nor I knew the finish. I remember asking NWA booker George Scott, 'What's going on?' And he told me, 'I haven't made up my mind yet.' He ran a couple of things by us—me winning, Flair winning, a draw, a disqualification, a run-in—and they all sounded good. No one knew the outcome until about an hour before the match."

Nearly the End

On October 4, 1975, Flair's career nearly ended when he was in a serious plane crash in Wilmington, North Carolina that took the life of the pilot and paralyzed wrestler Johnny Valentine, father of WWE Hall of Famer Greg "The Hammer" Valentine. Also on board the flight were "Mr. Wrestling I" Tim Woods, Bob Bruggers and promoter David Crockett. Flair broke his back in three places, and at age 26, doctors told him he would never wrestle again. However, Flair conducted a rigorous physical therapy schedule and triumphantly returned to the ring just six months later, where he resumed his now-legendary feud with Wahoo McDaniel in early 1976. The crash forced Flair to alter his wrestling style. Instead of relying on the power-based, high-impact brawling style that he was trying to master early on, he shifted to a more athletic, technical style that he would use throughout the rest of his career.

Timing Is Everything

The events that led to Steamboat's defection to the NWA from the WWF in 1989 demonstrate degree to which one can never say never in the wrestling industry. Steamboat's first three-year WWF stint culminated with *WrestleMania III* on March 29, 1987, where Steamboat and "Macho Man" Randy Savage competed in what many wrestlers consider the best match in WWF history. After 14:35 of blinding action, Steamboat captured the WWF Intercontinental Championship from Savage, gaining revenge for an injury Savage inflicted on Steamboat's larynx several months earlier. The highly influential match was considered an instant classic by both fans and critics and was named 1987's Match of the Year by both *Pro Wrestling Illustrated* and the *Wrestling Observer*. Steamboat's career prospects looked bright.

Several weeks after winning the Intercontinental Championship, Steamboat asked WWF owner Vince

McMahon for some time off to be with his wife Bonnie, who was expecting their first son, Richard, Jr. This did not sit well with WWF management, which had the intention of making Steamboat a long-term Intercontinental Champion. McMahon therefore ordered Steamboat to drop the belt on a card held on June 2, 1987. Initially, he was set to lose to "The Natural" Butch Reed, but when Reed arrived at the arena that day unable to compete, Steamboat instead lost the belt to The Honky Tonk Man. Steamboat's son was born later that month, and Honky went on to have a 15-month title reign.

Ricky came back in time for the first annual *Survivor Series* in November 1987. However, management was still bitter over his impromptu sabbatical from his first WWF run, and he was not pushed or given any meaningful feuds. Steamboat himself has implied in interviews that he was being punished for one-upping the Hogan-Andre main event at *WrestleMania III*. His last major WWF appearance was at *WrestleMania IV* in March 1988. Shortly thereafter, he announced his retirement. He signed with the NWA in 1989, and the rest is history.

Chapter Four

A Flair for the Gold

This is the greatest moment of my life!

–Ric Flair

The record-setting, 16-time former world champion "Nature Boy" Ric Flair's spectacular 59-minute, 26-second match-winning stint in the January 19, 1992, *Royal Rumble* stands the test of time not only because of the athleticism Flair displayed in the bout, but because the match itself remains to this day the most talked-about gimmick match of its kind.

Throughout the mid '80s and early '90s, wrestling promotions introduced a number of "novelty" events to the pay-per-view schedule in order to take advantage of the expanded audience.

In 1987, the NWA debuted its *Bunkhouse Stampede* pay-per-view event, headlined by a bunkhouse battle royal where all combatants would "come as they are," wearing jeans and cowboy boots and carrying in their hands bats, chains, spikes and any other bone-crushing or flesh-tearing instrument. That same year, the WWF created the *Survivor Series*, where teams of four or five wrestlers would compete in elimination matches. In 1993, the WWF brought the *King of the Ring* to pay-per-view, where wrestlers qualified to earn a spot to compete in an eight-man, one-night single elimination tournament with the winner crowned "the King."

But the *Royal Rumble* was the most popular of all these novelty events. The first 20-man *Royal Rumble* was broadcast on January 24, 1988, on the USA network in the United States. The next year the WWF staged its first ever 30-man *Royal Rumble* pay-per-view event at The Summit in Houston, Texas.

For modern fans, the *Royal Rumble* remains one of the most anticipated events on the wrestling calendar. It's the first stop on the road to *WrestleMania*, the SuperBowl of wrestling. But more importantly, it is the only time fans get a chance to see 30 of their favorite stars brawl for 60 minutes, bodies tumbling from the ring to the arena floor, arms and legs flying, until only one man is left standing.

That doesn't mean that the idea for the Rumble is new. Fans have reveled in rumble-like spectacles for over a century. The classic battle royal, for example, was a traditional gimmick match that always garnered special attention from spectators. A predecessor to the rumble, it's an idea taken from the world of boxing.

Prior to 1865, boxing cards would feature bouts between five or six blindfolded slaves. These bouts were soon dubbed "battle royals." The slaves would battle bare-fisted, with the sole survivor declared the winner. Some promoters would have the slaves battle until only two remained. Their blindfolds would then be removed, and they would go face-to-face until an outright winner was declared. Of course, the purse money was awarded not to the victorious slave but to his owner.

These matches were eventually outlawed after the abolition of slavery. But battle royals continued to be held underground, oftentimes in what were called "smokers," or illegal venues. Throughout much of the late 19th century and well into the 1930s, many a dollar was made and many a life was taken in these brutal contests. Ralph Ellison's classic 1952 novel *The Invisible Man* offers a vivid portrait of a young African American's horrific experiences as an unwilling participant in one of these underground battle royals.

Some boxers survived these abusive matches and, battling the odds, eventually established themselves among the ranks of professional boxers. The legendary Jack Johnson worked his way up from obscurity, winning several of these barbaric scraps, eventually becoming the first black boxer to win the heavyweight championship of the world, a title he held between 1908 and 1915. Documentary filmmaker Ken Burns explains: "...for more than 13 years, Jack Johnson was the most famous and the most notorious African American on Earth."

The evolution of the battle royal from brutally violent spectacle to a managed showcase for wrestlers took place in the 1960s. These new shows were particularly popular in Northern California. Promoter Roy Shire staged the first high-profile professional wrestling battle royal at San Francisco's famed Cow Palace in 1967. Honoring tradition, the African American star Bearcat Wright ousted Ray "The Crippler" Stevens to win this 18-man tussle.

Battle royals became a staple of wrestling cards throughout the 1970s and 1980s. Andre the Giant, often described as the king of battle royals, competed in his first over-the-top-rope brawl on an AWA card held on October 17, 1982.

WWF Hall of Famer Pat Patterson, best known to fans as one of Mr. McMahon's stooges during the celebrated Austin-McMahon feud of the late '90s, is credited with developing the concept of the *Royal Rumble* in the late '80s. Unlike the traditional battle royal, in which all the participants would begin the match in the ring, with the *Royal Rumble* two contestants would start the match, and the remaining 28 wrestlers would join in one-by-one at two-minute or 90-second intervals. This new twist extended the length of the match. It also allowed different kinds of wrestlers to strut their stuff. The bigger, brawnier wrestlers could still showcase their brawling skills as they always had in battle royals. But now the smaller, more athletic sports entertainers could also show off their cardiovascular conditioning.

In short, the multi-fighter attraction had finally come of age, evolving from the cruel, illegal and exploitative underground shoot-fight into the centerpiece of one of the most important events of the wrestling world's most popular promotion.

For a wrestler like Ric Flair, who prided himself on his marathon-style feats as NWA world champion in the 1980s, the *Royal Rumble* was the perfect gimmick match. Yet, few fans of the "60-Minute Man" in the '80s could ever have imagined that the NWA/WCW's most coveted star would ever compete in a WWF ring. Only something extraordinary could make Flair jump to the WWF. Well, something did happen, and the surrounding circumstances make Ric Flair's *Royal Rumble* win historically significant as well as unexpected.

Throughout the '80s, wrestling enthusiasts dreamed of the ultimate face-off: the WWF's Hulk Hogan versus the NWA's Ric Flair. Who would win? Who was truly the more dominant wrestler? Would the Hulkster's power-based offense and incredible resilience prove to be too much for the smaller "Slick" Ric? Or would the speedier Nature Boy overwhelm the slower muscle-bound Hogan, twist him in knots with his mat wrestling skills and outlast him by extending the match to 30 or 45 minutes? What tricks would the self-proclaimed "Dirtiest Player in the Game" have for the beloved gym-going, prayer-saying, vitamin-eating Hulkster? Fans salivated over the possibilities and dreamed of the day their fantasy would become reality.

Ric Flair's road to the WWF, the *Royal Rumble* and a possible dream feud with Hulk Hogan would be paved by a series of behind-the-scenes disputes between Flair and then WCW Executive Vice President Jim Herd. One of the most notorious backstage conflicts in wrestling history, Flair versus Herd would have a massive impact on both the WWF and NWA.

Not long after billionaire media mogul Ted Turner purchased the NWA-affiliated Jim Crockett Promotions (now known as World Championship

Wrestling) in 1988, Jim Herd had been a station manager at St. Louis TV station KPLR-TV. His station produced the extremely popular show, *Wrestling at the Chase*. At the time WCW executives offered him the position as WCW head, he was an executive at Pizza Hut.

From the get-go, he and Flair did not see eye-to-eye. Reflecting back on Herd's tenure in WCW, Flair does not mince words: "Jim Herd knew nothing about wrestling."

In order to compete with the WWF in the late '80s and early '90s, Herd wanted to update the more traditional WCW/NWA product by forcing wrestlers to adopt "cartoon-style" gimmicks. One such gimmick, which thankfully never made it to TV, was a tag-team called "The Hunchbacks." Herd's idea was that they would never be pinned because the humps on their backs would prevent their shoulders from touching the mat! Herd also planned a new look for Ric Flair. The new gimmick-happy chief envisioned the golden-haired legend with a shaved head and a Roman gladiator-style outfit. Flair refused, instead agreeing after discussions to update his look by cutting his famous golden locks. Upon seeing this, one WCW official commented, "After we change Flair's gimmick, why don't we go to Yankee Stadium and change Babe Ruth's number?"

"I didn't know how to take it!" confesses a candid Flair. "I was shocked and overwhelmed. It became a very trying period of time for me."

This aggressive approach cost WCW's talent roster dearly. No-nonsense grapplers like Stan "The Lariat" Hansen and The Road Warriors left WCW during Herd's tenure.

The backstage feud between Flair and Herd hit the breaking point in the weeks leading up to WCW's June 1991 event, *The Great American Bash*. Herd wanted the then WCW champion Flair to drop the title and subsequently take a pay cut and give up his main event spot to younger competitors. Flair, still the company's top draw, again refused.

Herd called Flair at his home in Charlotte, North Carolina. "Don't worry about it. We don't want ya!" screamed an always-aggressive Herd. He fired Flair, stripping him of the title belt. "I'm sending security over to pick up the belt," Herd added. Flair, who like all WCW/NWA champions until that point had left the company a $25,000 deposit for the belt, replied: "Tell them to bring the $25,000 plus interest!" "Stick it up you're a**, keep the belt," Herd blasted back. Flair did just that. What no one expected was that he also signed on with the WWF and took the belt with him. Once there, he billed himself the "Real World Champion."

Flair, relieved that his WCW career and Jim Herd were behind him, took on the hated Bobby

"The Brain" Heenan as his financial advisor and later "Mr. Perfect" Curt Hennig as his executive consultant. Commenting on his 1991–93 run in the WWF, Flair later stated: "I had the greatest year and a half of my career, outside my run in the NWA with the Four Horsemen."

Now in the WWF, Flair zeroed in on champion Hulk Hogan in the fall of 1991. Would the dream match actually happen?

Hogan was set to defend his title against the Undertaker at November's *Survivor Series*. Before the event, Flair, his Real World championship belt—the longtime emblem of the NWA—in hand, confronted Hogan on *The Funeral Parlor,* hosted by the Undertaker's manager, Paul Bearer. "You know how long I have been waiting for this very moment, big man?" a confident Flair began. The surrealistic sight of Hogan and Flair finally on the same stage left the fans in the arena in awe. "I've just burst that bubble you've been living in, and I'm here on your doorstep with the real world championship belt!" Mocking Hogan's catchphrase, Flair asked: "What are you gonna do, Hulk Hogan, when Ric Flair runs wild on you?"

WWF promoters set in motion a program that was to come to a head with Hogan facing Flair in the most anticipated match of the decade at *WrestleMania VIII* to be held five months later.

At the *Survivor Series,* Flair illegally assisted the Undertaker to defeat Hogan to win the title. Six days later, at the one-time pay-per-view event entitled *Tuesday in Texas,* Hogan threw ashes from the Undertaker's urn in his opponent's eyes to regain the belt. The events surrounding the second title change led WWF president Jack Tunney to order the WWF title vacant for only the second time in its history. The vacancy was to be filled in January 1992, with the winner of the *Royal Rumble* declared the undisputed champion.

The 1992 *Royal Rumble* would have gone down in history as an important one just for this lead up. But what sealed the importance of the 1992 *Royal Rumble* match was that, thanks to Flair's remarkable performance, it proved to be a cracking contest.

The match itself featured the greatest collection of talent ever assembled in a single ring: former AWA and WWF champion Sgt. Slaughter, former WWF champion "Macho Man" Randy Savage, Sid (Vicious) Justice, "British Bulldog" Davey Boy Smith, Hulk Hogan, The Undertaker, former AWA champ "The Model" Rick Martel, a young "Heartbreak Kid" Shawn Michaels, then WWF Intercontinental champ "Rowdy" Roddy Piper, Jake "The Snake" Roberts, and "Texas Tornado" Kerry Von Erich. They all had the WWF title gold on their minds. "If you look at that *Royal Rumble,* it was the Who's Who of wrestling," Flair pointed out some years later.

As always, a deciding factor in the success of a competitor in a rumble match is the luck of the draw—the number that would dictate when he'd enter the melee.

"It is now time for the *Royal Rumble!*" ring announcer Howard Finkel informed the sold-out crowd at Albany, New York's Knickerbocker Arena. "Let us all find out who drew number one for the *Royal Rumble!*"

Davey Boy Smith, hot on the heels of a battle royal win at the Royal Albert Hall in London a few months earlier, and "Million Dollar Man" Ted DiBiase, who lasted 47 minutes in the 1990 Rumble match, opened the contest at numbers one and two. DiBiase soon found himself sailing over the top rope before the number three entrant could make his appearance. The capacity crowd and a nervous color commentator, Bobby Heenan, looked over at the curtain with anticipation. "Who's number three?" asked an overwrought "Brain."

The two-minute timer counted down for the next entrant—"five, four, three, two, one."

"NO! D**n it!" blurted Heenan. Ric Flair marched through the curtain. "You can kiss him goodbye, Brain," play-by-play man Gorilla Monsoon screamed, irking an irate Heenan. "Never before in the history of the *Royal Rumble* has anyone who has drawn numbers one through five been there at the end!" "SHUT UP!" Heenan retorted. Flair's prospects looked dim.

He immediately found himself in trouble when the muscular Davey Boy countered his every hold with press slams and heavy-handed clotheslines.

Participant number four, the heel "Nasty Boy" Jerry Sags, helped Flair catch an early breather. Flair and Sags double-teamed the "British Bulldog" and looked as though they would form a temporary alliance. The Bulldog would have none of it. With a flying dropkick, Davey Boy eliminated Sags. He then turned to Flair and pointed: "It's you and me." "This isn't fair to Flair," begged Heenan.

As the Nature Boy and Davey Boy continued to brawl and the next several entrants made their way to the ring, it became apparent that Flair would be a target for each new participant. An increasingly desperate Heenan, hoping that some wrestler would help Flair, realized that it didn't matter who was set to come out next. "It does matter," replied Monsoon, continuing to be a thorn in The Brain's side, "some guys hate Flair more than others!"

Flair slouched in corners whenever he could, trying to catch his wind. Inevitably, as the minutes ticked away, he absorbed a great deal of punishment. He was backdropped and superkicked by

Shawn Michaels, subjected to "El Matador" Tito Santana's graceful flying forearm, Greg Valentine's lethal figure-four leglock and a brutal press slam by The Barbarian. Flair fought back with a slew of holds, some legal, some not—suplexes, chops, kicks and even eye gouges and low blows. Commenting on Flair's dirty tactics, Heenan quipped: "I'd do that to my grandmother if I had to!" The "Dirtiest Player in the Game" had only one goal in mind—winning—and would stoop to any level to get there.

When the buzzer rang signaling the ninth entrant, former NWA champ Kerry Von Erich, stepped through the curtain. The fans hit the roof. Von Erich and Flair had feuded in 1984. Flair, anxious to settle an old score, met the Texas Tornado head on. "Come on," Flair said, ushering Von Erich toward him. Von Erich cornered his tiring foe with a series of right hands and then spun around, connecting with his dreaded discus punch. Knocked silly, Flair marched out of the corner and flopped face-first onto the mat. He may have ducked some punches early in this bout, but as his confidence grew, Flair began to greet newcomers to the Rumble face-to-face.

One could sense that WWF fans, who had until this point been skeptical of Flair's skills, were developing respect for this man's moxy and conditioning.

When the hugely popular, 335-pound Big Boss Man hit the ring at number 13, eight other grapplers were battering one another in the ring. The Boss Man made a tour of the premises, unloading with jaw-rattling uppercuts. By this point, Davey Boy had been in the contest for an astonishing 22 minutes, Flair for 20.

In the words of WWE announcer Jim Ross, business was about to pick up.

With a shoulder dip, Flair eliminated both an exhausted Davey Boy Smith and Kerry Von Erich within 10 seconds of one another. One began to hear Flair's trademark "Whooooo!" ring throughout the crowd. Wrestlers dropped like flies, leaving Flair alone with the Boss Man. Attempting a high-risk cross-body block, Boss Man sailed over Flair and the top rope and found himself outside the ring. Once again a select group of fans cheered "Whoooo!"

Flair was the only man left in the ring. "Flair wins it, Flair is the champion of the world!" exploded Heenan prematurely. But only half of the Rumble's entrants had appeared. For Flair, the worst was yet to come.

As Flair curled into a ball in the middle of the ring, the countdown began again—"four, three, two, one..." Who would the next participant be?

Flair's worst nightmare: a fired-up "Hot Rod" Roddy Piper! The roof blew off the Knickerbocker

Arena. "Oh no, of all the people," pleaded The Brain. Flair's face winced as his eyes met up with his next challenger.

The Hot Scot showed no mercy, sprinting into the ring and leaping onto Flair, destroying him with a series of quick jabs, a backdrop and a monstrous flying knee-lift. The fans greeted every blow with a roar. Overwhelmed, Flair crawled under the bottom rope and outside the ring. Piper blasted him with a clothesline and rammed Flair's forehead into the metal guardrail. Back in the ring, Piper caught his archrival in a sleeper hold.

Flair was spent. And he would have found himself eliminated had entrant number 16, the treacherous Jake Roberts, not back-jumped Piper and saved Flair. "Thank you, Jake, thank you," groveled Heenan. Roberts turned around and short-clotheslined a glassy-eyed Nature Boy. "You can't trust a snake!" exclaimed Heenan.

For fans, the anticipation started to build—when would Hogan hit the ring? Prior to the event, President Jack Tunney had announced that Hogan and The Undertaker would receive special treatment in the draw, entering the ring only after the 20th spot. Their time was coming, and Flair knew that if he was going to last, he still had an uphill climb ahead.

Even as the "Hacksaw" Duggans and Jimmy "Superfly" Snukas entered the fracas and battered

Flair, Flair, who had been in the Rumble nearly 40 minutes, continued to fire back, dishing out punishment to opponents who were far fresher than he.

The Undertaker made his way to the ring at number 20, and despite owing his recent WWF title reign to Flair, immediately wrapped his gloved hand around "Slick" Ric's throat and choked him half unconscious. It truly was every man for himself.

"The Model" Rick Martel, who in the 1991 Rumble had lasted an astonishing 52 minutes and 17 seconds, entered at number 25 and nearly succeeded in dumping Flair out of the ring with a fireman's carry.

Flair continued to weather storm after storm.

"Please let him win it—please, I'll do anything," Heenan pleaded. "Will you stop begging!" screamed Monsoon.

Finally, the Hulkster was up! Fueled by the notion of becoming five-time WWF champion, Hogan slid under the bottom rope and cleaned house. He went right after Flair, hammering him with heavy rights to the fans' delight. By this point Flair had been in the ring for over three-quarters of an hour. The Undertaker interrupted the long anticipated clash, but after a stiff clothesline from Hogan, soon found his hopes of regaining his title dashed. The stoic Undertaker rolled his eyes back in his head in frustration.

Hogan once again set his sights on Flair, who amazingly responded with an eye-rake and a chop. "Can you believe this, the guy's still punching?" asked Monsoon, now impressed with Flair's athleticism. Hogan was impervious to the pain and stared down a decimated Flair. Just when Hogan was about to eliminate him with a bodyslam, Flair desperately grabbed onto Hogan's leg and, once again finding lady luck on his side, was saved by Irwin R. Schyster, who interrupted the Hulkster's momentum with an eye gouge.

Participants number 28 and 29, Sgt. Slaughter and Sid Justice, like many before them, took their shots at Flair, but the tenacious Nature Boy refused to let up.

Outlasting the later Rumble entries, Flair found himself in the final three with Hogan and Justice. Had he been eliminated at that point, his would have been a legendary performance. But Flair was not done yet.

As Hogan kicked a grounded Flair, Justice, until then a fan-favorite, approached Hogan from behind and threw Hogan over the top rope. Fans were astonished. As Justice and Hogan exchanged words, a gasping Flair, tired and beaten, saw his opening. He mustered up his last breath, hooked

Justice from behind and lifted him over the top rope.

"Yes, yes, yes, yes, yes!" rejoiced Heenan. "Flair did it!" Gorilla Monsoon confirmed.

The ring announcer Finkel made the official announcement: "The winner of the *Royal Rumble* and undisputed World Wrestling Federation champion, Ric Flair!"

Even for a legendary performer like Flair, this was an outstanding feat. Wrestling for a then record-setting 59 minutes and 26 seconds and outlasting 29 other combatants, Flair was on top of the wrestling world, the king of the mountain. He truly was "the 60-Minute Man."

In a classic post-match interview, Flair acknowledged the importance of this victory to his career, which, despite the setbacks of 1991, now looked as bright as ever. "I'm gonna tell you all with a tear in my eye, this is the greatest moment in my life." He then shocked the wrestling world by holding up the WWF belt and announcing: "This is the only title in the wrestling world that makes you number one! When you are the king of the WWF, you rule the world!" Loyal NWA/WCW fans must have felt crushed to hear "their boy" say this. And they owed it all to Jim Herd.

Flair now seemed set for an epic confrontation almost a decade in the making where he would likely lose the WWF title to Hogan at *WrestleMania*. But it was not to be. Hogan decided that he wanted to take a hiatus from wrestling, thus throwing a monkey wrench in the WWF's plans. Fans would have to wait until Hogan's equally unfathomable jump to WCW and *Bash at the Beach 1994* for the first-ever high-profile match between these two '80s icons.

MAT FACTS

Whacked In and Whacked Out

The record for the shortest-lived entrant in a *Royal Rumble* is the 330-pound Warlord, who in 1989 was ejected in just three seconds. The runner up is Bushwhacker Luke, who in 1991 hit the floor 4.8 seconds after entering the fray.

Luck of the Draw?

More Rumble winners have drawn the number 27 than any other entry slot. Big John Studd, Yokozuna, Bret Hart and Steve Austin each won a *Royal Rumble* as the 27th entrant. Despite being the last entry slot, the wrestler who has drawn 30 has only been victorious once. That win went to the Undertaker in 2007.

The Fairer Sex Wants In

The Ninth Wonder of the World Chyna was the first and only woman to ever be in a *Royal Rumble* match. She entered 30th in the 1999 Rumble and managed to eliminate Mark Henry, though she only lasted 35 seconds. She also participated in the 2000 Rumble match.

Royal Rumble King

Steve Austin has the most *Royal Rumble* victories, winning the 1997, 1998 and 2001 Rumbles. He has also made more eliminations overall than anyone else with 36, followed by Shawn Michaels (31), Kane (29) and The Undertaker (29).

Dark Matches

The original plans for Flair to battle Hogan at *Wrestle-Mania VIII* fell through, and their first high-profile battle was on July 17, 1994, in WCW. But Hogan and Flair actually met in WWF rings in the fall of 1991. The first ever Hogan vs. Flair contest took place on October 25, 1991, in Oakland, California. No one outside the local market saw the match take place. They also fought "dark matches" at a sold out Boston Garden and a nearly packed Madison Square Garden as well.

Chapter Five

Home Is Where the Hart Is

*It was a really interesting time, and I thought it
was a fun time for wrestling fans, too.*
                                    –Bret "The Hitman" Hart

To the dismay of the 20,593 rabid Montreal fans
watching the *Survivor Series* from ringside,
challenger Shawn Michaels had hooked then WWF
champion Bret "The Hitman" Hart in the sharpshooter. What happened next was not on the script,
as far as Bret Hart knew. On the orders of WWF
owner Vince McMahon, who had for some reason
made his way to ringside flanked by several officials,
referee Earl Hebner called for the bell to ring. Bret
hadn't tapped out. Bret hadn't squealed, "I quit."
But the match was over. Michaels, with whom Bret
had had a notoriously acrimonious relationship
behind the scenes for years, nervously grabbed the

title belt and was promptly escorted back to the dressing area.

Bret couldn't believe it. He spat in McMahon's face and went on a rampage, destroying $50,000 television monitors at ringside. As the confused live crowd filed out of the Molson Centre buzzing, Bret was joined in the ring by his brother Owen and his brother-in-law Davey Boy Smith, who whispered into Bret's ear. The crowd that remained cheered as Bret drew the letters W-C-W in the air with his finger. But none of this would be enough to quell The Hitman's rage.

With his son Blade at his side, Bret undressed backstage in the same room as Shawn Michaels. "Shawn, you weren't in on that?" a suspicious and shell-shocked Hart asked. "I had no f*****g idea…. As God is my f*****g witness," Michaels answered. "My hands are clean of this one, I swear to God."

Michaels was lying.

In fact, McMahon had confided in Michaels about his plans to double-cross Bret and to relieve him of the title some time before the match. Bret had signed a contract with WCW at Vince's request prior to the *Survivor Series* when the WWF owner admitted that, due to financial difficulties, he would not be able to honor the 20-year, multi-million-dollar contract Bret had signed with the WWF. But when Bret refused to drop the title in Canada for fear that it would hurt the reputation of his "Hitman" character as a Canadian hero, McMahon became concerned that Bret would be coaxed by WCW promoters to bring the WWF title belt to the rival company and pitch it in a rubbish bin. This was not a risk McMahon was willing to take.

"What would you want to do today, then?" Bret asked Vince in a meeting the day of the match, to which Vince responded, "I've been trying to rack my brain thinking about the finish." "I mean, I don't have to beat Shawn," Bret explained. "We could have a schmoz, or whatever you want. I think it allows me a chance to leave with my head up and leave in a nice way." "Whatever you want," Vince complied. "Okay," said Bret.

Hart wanted to have the *Survivor Series* match end in a wild brawl. He would drop the title to Shawn weeks later on U.S. soil. Vince appeared to agree. But as Bret and Vince were butting heads over the match's finish, Vince secretly devised a plan that would protect the WWF Championship.

Moments after Bret interrogated Shawn, Vince appeared outside Bret's dressing room. He wanted to talk to Bret. They chatted for several minutes, after which Vince re-emerged from the dressing room groggy, stumbling, his eye red and swelling. "I drilled him, as hard as I could," Bret told a documentary filmmaker who recorded the events. "It knocked him right out. And I told him to get out."

The events of November 9, 1997, remain controversial for wrestling insiders and fans. Opinions are
split: was Bret screwed, or did Vince do what he
had to do? What's absolutely clear is that in the
immediate aftermath of the WWF's 11th annual
Survivor Series pay-per-view, the vast majority of
fans sympathized with The Hitman. Canadians felt
slighted. In a poll taken just after the event,
75 percent of Canadian wrestling fans said that
they would watch less or no WWF as a result of
what had already become known as the "Montreal
Screw Job." (Ironically, the WWF became more
popular as a result of the uproar.)

In McMahon's famous "Bret screwed Bret" speech
on the November 17, 1997, edition of *Raw*, the
WWF owner showed no remorse for his actions,
demonstrating no sympathy for Hart and blaming
the Canadian star alone for the events that marred
his departure from the WWF. In response, Bret Hart
stated: "What he did with me in the *Survivor Series*
was a total lack of respect for my fans, my fellow
wrestlers and me. I worked for the WWF for 14 years
and gave this man the greatest performances in
the history of the game, having only missed two
shows in 14 years, having been a leader inside
and outside the dressing room. And for Vince
McMahon to lie to me and cheat me for no reason
at all, other than his own paranoid delusions,
shows what kind of a man he really is. Vince
McMahon screwed Bret."

Hart claimed that he would never consider returning to the WWF/WWE. He made his debut for WCW on a December 15 edition of *Nitro*, making only a passing reference to Montreal. In the WWF, McMahon and company made November 7 the centerpiece of its shows for weeks, using it to establish what would become Vince's extremely successful heel owner character.

So ended Bret Hart's fifth WWF title reign and his WWF career.

What makes the controversial events surrounding his departure so surprising is that Bret Hart had reached his peak as a performer and was a key element in WWF's effort to compete with WCW in the Monday Night Wars of 1997. Indeed, he had arguably delivered some of his best performances in the ring and on the mike during this period.

Most memorable of all was Hart's feud with anti-hero babyface "Stone Cold" Steve Austin. As their rivalry heated up, Hart and Austin enlisted the help of other wrestlers. Hart formed the pro-Canadian faction, the Hart Foundation. Outnumbered and often falling victim to some brutal beat-downs at the hands of Hart's henchmen, Austin responded by forming an uneasy pact with fellow true-blue American wrestlers sick of the Hart Foundation's gang-like tactics. This feud made the WWF essential viewing during the summer of 1997. The *Wrestling*

Observer Newsletter crowned the feud the best in wrestling for that year.

This incredible feud culminated with a truly unforgettable, near-half-hour 10-man tag-team main event that many experts regard as one of the greatest in WWF history. That match took place as part of *In Your House: Canadian Stampede* on July 6, 1997.

In the weeks and months leading up to the Stampede, Bret Hart had taken the top spot in the WWF and was famous as a pro-Canadian, anti-American heel. For fans familiar with his earlier career, his new stance would come as a surprise.

The Hitman's transformation and march to the top of the WWF began with his spectacular *WrestleMania XIII* submission victory over "Stone Cold" Steve Austin on March 23, 1997. During that contest, the two wrestlers "switched spots," as they say in wrestling parlance. Austin had entered the match as a cheap-shotting rule breaker, and Bret was the straight-laced babyface. But by the end of their *WrestleMania* contest, everything had reversed. Bret was vehemently booed by the Chicago crowd, and Austin was cheered for his hard-edged, bird-flipping attitude. This was only the beginning of what would become a major feud.

The fans forced the hand of the promoters in this case. The fans had chosen Austin over Bret as their favorite. Although Bret would have preferred to remain a fan favorite, he knew that Austin's popularity was growing. "You can't resist it," he commented later. But he wasn't making a sacrifice. He knew that the popularity of his "Hitman" character had never been greater north of the 49th parallel and overseas. A unique opportunity presented itself, and he moved to exploit it.

In a post-*WrestleMania* promo, The Hitman lashed out at fans—but not all fans. Just the American ones. First, he apologized for his recent actions, but then he began to take swipes at Americans. "First of all, I want to apologize…to all my fans over in Germany, to all great fans over in Great Britain, actually I'd like to apologize to all my fans all over Europe. But I'd especially like to apologize to all my great fans in Canada. And to you, my fans across the United States of America, I apologize for nothing! It seems really strange to me that no matter how much I tried, that when I beat 'Stone Cold' Steve Austin to a bloody pulp, when I walked back to the dressing room the way you American fans treated me across the United States of America, I felt like I lost," Bret complained, belittling the red, white and blue audience. "It's obvious to me that you American wrestling fans from coast-to-coast don't respect me. Well, the fact is I don't respect you. So from here on in, the American fans from coast-to-coast can kiss my a**!" These words instantaneously mobilized Canadian fan-support for Calgary's favorite son.

A North American war was declared with Hart spearheading an anti-U.S.A. campaign.

"It was a really interesting time, and I thought it was a really fun time for wrestling fans, too," reminisced Bret. "I always felt funny saying the things I said about Americans. But at the same time, I was happy to allow the Canadian fans to find a hero in me. The wrestling fans in the States wanted to play a role: they wanted to be the bad guys!"

Generally, wrestling fans tend to respond more or less uniformly to wrestlers and storylines—"bad guys" are jeered, "good guys" are cheered. But in this case, the WWF fan base was split along the U.S.–Canadian border. "That was the first time we had a Canadian contingent that was cheered overwhelmingly in Canada and booed like hell in the United States," remembers Vince McMahon.

As the summer months unfolded, Bret formed the ultimate Canadian heel stable, The Hart Foundation, borrowing the name from his former tag team combination with Jim "The Anvil" Neidhart. Standing alongside Hart and Neidhart were "The Loose Cannon" Brian Pillman, a former Calgary Stampeder; Owen Hart; and Davey Boy Smith. One fan at a Canadian edition of *Raw* proudly held up a poster depicting all five members of the Hart Foundation relieving themselves on the Star-Spangled Banner.

The WWF rode this angle to success, packing houses from Edmonton, Alberta, to San Antonio, Texas, from Halifax, Nova Scotia, to Pittsburgh, Pennsylvania. In Edmonton, on July 7, Bret proudly sported an Edmonton Oilers jersey and thanked Canadian fans for their loyalty. "Thank you for still letting me be your hero, and for still believin' in me. A few weeks ago, I was told, 'America, love it or leave it.' I've been all over the United States of America, and the one thing I've particularly looked forward to is lovin' leavin' it!" The Edmonton horde cheered. "To me, Canada is a country where we still take care of the sick and the old, where we still have health care, where we have gun control—we don't shoot each other and kill each other on every street corner. Canada isn't riddled with racial prejudice and hatred. Across Canada we all care for each other. And I am proud to be a Canadian. And I am proud to be your hero!"

Hart's masterful verbal performances cut differently with American crowds.

He reserved his most passionate vitriol for Pittsburgh, where he cut his now-famous "enema" speech. "Last week, I said that the United States of America was one, big, giant toilet bowl," he spurted, as the crowd booed and chanted "U-S-A, U-S-A." in defiance. "If you were going to give the United States of America an enema, you'd stick the hose right here in Pittsburgh, Pennsylvania!" With this line, Bret Hart morphed into one of the most hated men in wrestling.

Austin, for his part, started hearing more and more cheers from American fans. He represented what they wanted to be: a crude, bird-flipping, anti-establishment beer-guzzler who got his way by any means necessary. In the late '90s, being an American no longer meant being a straight-laced, prayer-saying, selfless hero. The Hulk Hogans and the Bret Harts—the heroes of the '80s and early '90s—didn't represent what it took to get ahead in the "real" world. A no-frills, foul-mouthed, rule-breaking opportunist like Austin did. For these reasons, he hit a nerve with the blue-collar masses. Never was this attitude on better display than during his most famous promo, which he cut just minutes after winning the *King of the Ring* tournament in June 1996. After defeating born-again Christian and sentimental favorite Jake "The Snake" Roberts in the final round, Austin blasted his downed foe, to the delight of fans: "You sit there and you thump your Bible, and you say your prayers, and it didn't get you anywhere! Talk about your Psalms, talk about John 3:16...Austin 3:16 says I just whipped your a**!" As the feud with Hart unfolded, Hart painted Austin as the epitome of American crudeness, as an emblem of the way America selfishly and violently bullies the rest of the world. Austin reveled in his ability to antagonize Bret. He once said: "If you put the letter 'S' in front of 'Hitman,' you have my exact opinion of Bret Hart."

A highlight of the Hart Foundation-Austin feud in the months before the *Canadian Stampede* event was an unsanctioned Street Fight between Hart and Austin on the April 21 edition of *Raw*. As both men battled in jeans and steel-toed boots, Austin smashed Hart's knee with a steel chair to the American fans' delight.

As the match continued, Austin locked Hart in Hart's signature sharpshooter submission hold. Austin held the lethal leglock for two-plus minutes as WWF officials filled the ring trying to save The Hitman. Seriously injured, Hart was carted away on a stretcher, consoled by Hart Foundation members and, once backstage, wheeled into an ambulance, his face wincing in pain. It was a top-notch perfor-mance. Unbeknownst to Foundation members and fans alike, Austin had commandeered the vehicle, occupying the driver's seat. The scintillating angle unfolded as Austin popped out of driver's seat, screaming, "I told you we're going straight to hell!" He proceeded to brutalize Hart further as he lay strapped to the gurney. "It was one of the best shows they ever did," commented Hart.

Reflecting on the match, Hart gave some insight into the motivations of his character. "The fans loved it," he explained. "But when you put yourself in the shoes of my character, you think what a bunch of cold-blooded people that they would turn their backs on me and cheer him on to do that to me and end my career. That was really the underlying premise throughout this angle: my character represented what was right." And yet, the anti-hero Austin was cheered!

In the long term, Austin, the lone wolf Texan, was outnumbered five-to-one by the Hart Foundation. So he reluctantly agreed to join forces with Goldust, The Legion of Doom (L.O.D.) and Ken Shamrock, each of whom had had their own troubles with Hart's gang. Somehow, some way, Austin and crew wanted to get even with the Canadian faction. They would get their opportunity on July 6 in a 10-man tag match. But their prospects didn't look promising. The match would take place in the house the Harts built, the Calgary Saddledome, before a partisan crowd of 12,151.

From the perspective of today's wrestling fan, it all seems to make perfect sense. The Harts, trained as traditional wrestlers in Stu Hart's legendary Dungeon in the Hart family home, represented the family unit and got a warm hometown welcome. The outlaw Texan in black, who cussed and two-timed foes and friends alike, was subjected to a chorus of hisses. That's the way the wrestling world has always worked.

But in the WWF of 1997, in a world where, for the time being, the distinction between heel and babyface had become—to borrow a phrase from the opening segment of *Canadian Stampede*—"a canvas of muted greys." It all took on new meaning. Austin and Bret, the blood rivals, were in fact mirror images of one another. But on this day, the evil Harts became heroes for a day.

After the playing of "O Canada" and with the entire Hart family (an 80-year old Stu included) sitting in the front row, the Calgary crowd was at a fever pitch. Austin and Bret began the match with a nose-to-nose stare down. Davey Smith, Owen Hart, Brian Pillman and Jim Neidhart stood proudly in the Hart Foundation corner. Ken Shamrock, Goldust and the L.O.D. paced in the other. They were all itching for the melee to get underway.

Hart and Austin's initial exchange saw Bret receive an overwhelming response from the crowd for every move he connected. The Saddledome shook as Hart battered Austin in the corner with unanswered punches and kicks.

"This building is shaking!" squawked color man, Jerry "The King" Lawler.

A low blow and a bargain-basement eye-rake with the bootlaces changed the tide. Austin followed up with a Million Dollar Dream sleeperhold, hoping to put Hart out. Hart kicked off a turnbuckle and flipped over, knotting Stone Cold up in a pinning combination that nearly ended the match early.

Bret tagged in former three-time WWF tag champ "The Anvil" to some fanfare. Austin quickly took his burly opponent down with a Lou Thesz press.

Several tags were made before Brian Pillman and UFC standout Ken Shamrock matched holds. The grinning, diabolical former Cincinnati Bengal peppered Shamrock with bites, spits and chops.

Yet another series of tags saw the current Intercontinental champ Owen Hart meet Goldust head-on. The raucous audience greeted the champ with a lively chant of "O-wen, O-wen." He blasted Dusty Rhodes' eldest son with a hard *insiguri* kick to the back of the head. The smooth-flowing action continued at a breakneck pace.

The boisterous Canadians rumbled the rafters: "Austin sucks! Austin sucks!" The atmosphere was red hot!

When Bret connected with a suspiciously low boot on Goldust, play-by-play announcer Vince McMahon called it right: "I guess the Harts can do no wrong here in Calgary!" "I guess not," continued Lawler, "that was Bret Hart's mother, Helen Hart, leading the chant that 'Austin sucks'!"

When Goldust found himself staked out in the Hart Foundation corner, viciously quintuple-teamed and force-fed kick after kick, Austin and Shamrock barged in. The official quickly restored order.

With so much at stake and so many egos involved, the match predictably broke out into a 10-man brawl. During the melee, Austin blasted Owen's knee with a chair-shot so hard that the younger Hart had to be helped to the back. One of the Harts sitting in the front row, former wrestler Bruce Hart, couldn't stomach it, grabbing hold of Austin's tights and hammering him with clubbing blows. Pulling away, Austin seemed to relish every second of the ensuing "Austin sucks!" chant.

Owen Hart's injury turned out to be a turning point. Finding themselves down four men against five, the fan favorite Harts had an uphill battle to fight. But Bret was determined to cut the competition down to size. After Austin nailed Pillman with a Stone Cold Stunner, Bret pulled Austin's leg over to the corner and retaliated for his brother by destroying Austin's knee, first with a fire extinguisher and then with a brutal figure four around the iron ring post. Yet another competitor bit the dust as officials accompanied Austin to the dressing area.

The remaining eight wrestlers continued to battle until Pillman fired Shamrock into a ringside table. Chaos ensued once again!

Moments after Davey Boy lifted Goldust over for a whopping superplex and earned a two-and-a-half count, a stubborn Austin hobbled back to the ring.

There's no way that the "Rattlesnake" was going to miss this fight!

Tags on each team left Bret and Austin once again one-on-one. This time Austin gained the advantage with a flurry of rights and kicks in the corner. "There has never before been a match quite like this one!" exclaimed McMahon.

Although The Hitman countered with a spinning neckbreaker and his patented backbreaker-elbowdrop combination, a one-legged Austin eventually made Hart cry out in pain with a sharpshooter. But this match was far from over.

Owen Hart valiantly dragged himself back to the ring and broke the hold just in time.

Owen and Austin then trickled to the floor where Austin decided to take a swipe at the Hart patriarch, Stu himself. As the crowd exploded, the Hart clan at ringside, Stu included, mauled Stone Cold. Bret managed to throw Austin back in the ring, but Austin allowed his concentration to lapse, whereupon Owen quickly rolled up Austin for the match-deciding three-count.

Pandemonium reigned for several minutes. Members of the Hart family stormed the ring where they outnumbered the fallen American contingent. Then, just as the skirmish appeared about to subside, Austin stormed the ring one last time with a steel chair in hand. "That Rattlesnake is not afraid of anything!" screamed announcer Jim Ross. The Hart Foundation and company once again mauled him.

Austin was swiftly handcuffed and forcibly removed by security—spitting, cursing and kicking all the way. He also made sure to let the lively Saddledome crowd know how he felt, shooting them a two-handed one-finger salute.

One of the wildest shootouts in WWF history was over.

As the dust settled, Stu and Helen joined the entire Hart clan in the ring for a touching celebration. Not a single fan left the Saddledome. No one in attendance wanted to miss the opportunity to praise Canada's first family of wrestling in its finest hour.

"All of Canada is proud of the first family of the World Wrestling Federation," commented McMahon, to which Ross added: "This is a very special moment in this industry!"

This match—like all great matches—left fans wanting more. American fans were anxious for Austin to even the score. For Austin, the *Canadian Stampede* tag match and the feud with the Hart Foundation proved to be a vital steppingstone. One year later, he'd be the biggest name in the game.

Bret would win his last WWF title victory against the Undertaker at *SummerSlam '97* one month later. Five months after that, the "Montreal Screw-job" would throw his entire career into question. But it couldn't tarnish his world-class performance during the summer of 1997.

MAT FACTS

Never Say Never

After some years of on-and-off negotiation, Bret Hart finally returned to the WWE television network when he was inducted into the WWE Hall of Fame, Class of 2006. Hart did not appear the next day at *WrestleMania 22* with the 2006 Hall of Fame inductees at the Allstate Arena in Chicago, Illinois, saying that he didn't feel "comfortable with the situation."

This Gun's For You

Brian Pillman became a controversial competitor in the final years of his career. His "Loose Canon" moniker was well deserved. On the November 4, 1996, episode of *Monday Night Raw*, Pillman took part in the infamous "Pillman's got a gun" angle with Steve Austin. Austin and Pillman had been feuding for several weeks, and Austin had finally decided to take matters into his own hands and visit an injured Pillman at home. WWF interviewer Kevin Kelly sat in Pillman's house with a camera crew and the Pillman family while Pillman's friends surrounded the house to protect him. Austin was attacked by Pillman's friends as soon as he arrived but made it past them. He then proceeded to break into Pillman's home and made a motion to attack Pillman.

But Pillman produced the same 9 mm Glock that he had displayed earlier and pointed it at a hesitant Austin. Kelly and Pillman's wife Melanie screamed for help. The satellite feed was then disrupted, and the scene went black. The on-scene director contacted commentator Vince McMahon and reported that he had heard "a couple explosions." The transmission was restored shortly before the end of *Raw,* and viewers witnessed Pillman's friends dragging Austin from the house while Pillman aimed the gun at him and announced his intention to "kill that son of a b***h!" Pillman also slipped up, saying "f***" on live television where it could not be edited out. The WWF (and Pillman personally) eventually apologized profusely for the entire angle, with Pillman claiming that the profanity "just slipped out."

The Departed

Four of the 10 men who competed at the *Calgary Stampede* main event have since died. Brian Pillman, born Brian William Pillman, died of a previously undetected heart condition—atherosclerotic heart disease—on October 5, 1997. He was 35. Thirty-four-year old Owen Hart passed away on May 23, 1999. Davey Boy Smith, whose middle name was, in fact, "Boy" (his parents confused the middle name field on his birth certificate for the gender field) died of a heart attack on May 18, 2002 at age 39, after years of consuming steroid cocktails and human growth hormones. And Legion of Doom/Road Warrior Hawk, born Michael Hegstrand, passed away on October 19, 2003, also of a heart attack. At 46 years of age, he had just bought a condominium and overcome his addiction to alcohol and recreational drugs.

Since 1985, the death rate among wrestlers has been alarmingly high. A *USA Today* article published on March 12, 2004, showed that 1000 men younger than 46 had participated in pro wrestling over a seven-year period and that at least 65 of them had died in that time, 25 from some type of coronary disease. The story chronicled widespread steroid use in the ring plus extensive use of painkillers. The article claimed that between 1997 and 2004 pro wrestlers were 20 times more likely to die by age 45 than pro football players.

Here is a list of some of the youngest wrestlers to die since 1985:

NAME	AGE
Chris Von Erich	21
Mike Von Erich	23
Louie Spiccol	27
Art Barr	28
Jay Youngblood	30
Buzz Sawyer	32
Crash Holly	32
Kerry Von Erich	33
Eddie Gilbert	33
The Renegade	33
Chris Candido	33
Adrian Adonis	34
Gary Albright	34
Bobby Duncum Jr.	34
Yokozuna	34
Pitbull #2	36
Eddie Guerrero	38
John Kronus	38
Johnny Grunge	39
Vivian Vachon	40
Terry Gordy	40
Bertha Faye	40
Chris Benoit	40
Rick Rude	41
Bruiser Brody	42
Miss Elizabeth	42
Big Boss Man	42
Earthquake	42
Mike Awesome	42
Nancy Benoit (Woman)	43
Dino Bravo	44
Curt Hennig	44
Bam Bam Bigelow	45
Jerry Blackwell	45
Junkyard Dog	45
Hercules	45
Andre the Giant	46
Big John Studd	46
Dick Murdoch	49
Jumbo Tsuruta	49
Rocco Rock	49
"Sensational" Sherri Martel	49
Moondog Spot	51
Uncle Elmer	54
Eddie Graham	55
Haystacks Calhoun	55
Giant Haystacks	55
The Spoiler	56
Gene Anderson	58
Dr. Jerry Graham	58
Bulldog Brown	58
Ray Stevens	60
Stan Stasiak	60
Terry Garvin	60
Little Beaver	61
Sapphire	61
Shohei Baba	61
Dick the Bruiser	62
Wilbur Snyder	62
Gorilla Monsoon	62
Bad News Brown	63
Wahoo McDaniel	63

Chapter Six

To Hell and Back

As God is my witness, he is broken in half!
　　　　　　　　　　　　　　－Jim Ross

The official laundry list of injuries reads as follows: a dislocated jaw , a dislocated shoulder, a bruised kidney, two broken ribs, one and a half missing teeth, a concussion and 14 stitches for the cut beneath his lip. It took him two months to recover. But some of the injuries have never fully healed.

Mick "Mankind" Foley—the man, the wrestler—would never be the same again after the beating he received from the Undertaker. His injuries also revealed how horribly real a "fake" wrestling match can sometimes become.

Mankind's battle with The Undertaker on June 28, 1998, before a packed house of 17,087 at the

"Igloo" in Pittsburgh, Pennsylvania, will surely go down in history as the most brutal, stunt-filled steel cage match in wrestling history. It is also emblematic of the WWF's late '90s Attitude Era. Appropriately, the tagline for that year's *King of the Ring* event was "Off With Their Heads."

Foley's injuries, while unusually severe, are not uncommon. Cracked ribs, deep cuts, internal bleeding, broken necks—there are hundreds of stories of horrific injuries and gruesome mishaps occurring in the ring.

For example, on a July 17, 1999, card held by the Japanese promotion, Michinoku Pro, The Great Sasuke locked horns with a wrestler by the name of The Dirt Bike Kid. The Kid dominated the contest until, suddenly, Sasuke lost his cool, ditched the prearranged script and began to batter the Kid. He belted his opponent with 18 full-force kicks and then choked him into unconsciousness to win the match. Weeks later, Kid commented on his loss: "I received a kick to the ribs which basically broke the cartilage on the right side of my chest which connects the ribs to my sternum." It put an end to his career. Today, The Dirt Bike Kid is nowhere to be found in the wrestling industry.

Another Japanese wrestler, Yukihiro Kanemura, of the Japanese W*ING league, was famous for doing anything to win over fans. In March 1993, at the ripe age of 21, he paid a visit to the now defunct southern U.S.-based Smokey Mountain Wrestling (SMW) promotion for a match with grizzled psychopath Kevin Sullivan. In their match, Kanemura allowed himself to be knifed repeatedly with a metal spike to the forehead and forearm. When the match was broadcast, SMW officials were forced to place a giant "X" across the screen. The injuries incurred required 58 stitches, many of which had to be inserted beneath the skin to repair the underlying muscular tissue. Another wrestler remembered the match: "It's about the most blood I've ever seen. I remember his bone sticking out."

On an independent card in Helsinki, Finland, on September 27, 2003, a wrestler by the name of Alan Funk (formerly "Kwee Wee" of WCW fame) suffered an appalling injury after his foe, Sonny Siaki, missed a split-legged moonsault. Siaki whacked Funk in the face with his knees, leaving him with a fractured skull, a broken nose, a broken orbital bone, a jaw broken in two places and a perforated eardrum. Realizing how much blood he was losing, Funk sprinted back-stage only to discover that one of his eyeballs was hanging out of its socket. Although doctors told him he would not live through the night, Funk survived. Five surgeries later, he has partial vision in his right eye, but still no hearing in his left ear. Amazingly, he returned to action for the All-Japan company in the fall of 2004.

The most memorable injury suffered by any wrestler on a U.S. mainstream event was surely when Sid Vicious snapped his leg clean in half during WCW's *Sin* pay-per-view on January 14, 2001. This truly sickening spectacle occurred during a match pitting Sid against Scott Steiner, Jeff Jarrett and Road Warrior Animal in a Fatal Four-Way. Normally a lumbering, muscle-bound goon, Sid decided to ascend to the second rope to deliver a thunderous kick to an opponent. He landed awkwardly, and his fibula and tibia simultaneously gave way under his weight. Sid required a two-hour operation the next day, which included inserting a 43 centimeter-long metal rod below the kneecap to reset his leg. He returned to the ring in June 2004 for a match in Montreal, Quebec.

Prior to entering the WWF and in the lead up to his match with the Undertaker, Mick "Mankind" Foley had quite the reputation as a violent competitor. Originally known as Cactus Jack, the wild man from Truth or Consequences, New Mexico, Foley and Maxx Payne faced off against the notoriously reckless Nasty Boys in WCW in 1994. All four men worked hard to produce a gripping series of pay-per-view matches. The first, on February 20 at *SuperBrawl IV*, saw Foley take a brutal bump off the ring apron onto the unprotected concrete floor (which caused him to cough blood). One of the Nastys' shoulders was dislocated with a bungled belly-to-back suplex by Payne, and Payne suffered a concussion when he was hit hard with a guitar-shot to the head. Foley once called this bout a "six-car pile-up on the freeway" rather than a wrestling match.

What made Foley's injuries in his match against the Nasty Boys—and much later against the Undertaker—different from the rest of these mishaps was that he voluntarily endured pain and suffering in order to give his fans a rise and get ahead in his career. The violence earned him respect. He was affectionately referred to by fans as "the Hardcore Legend." Ric Flair also famously dubbed him "a glorified stunt man." But neither of these nicknames really captures the ups and downs Foley experienced before, during and after his now-classic encounter with The Undertaker.

The WWF presented its first Hell in a Cell steel cage match on October 5, 1997, in St. Louis, Missouri in front of 21,151 fans at its *In Your House: Badd Blood* pay-per-view event. As the storyline went, the Undertaker devised the demonic Cell structure in order to inflict the greatest amount of pain on Shawn Michaels, the "Heartbreak Kid." (The two had been feuding since late August.) This new cage surrounded and covered the entire ring and stood an impressive 16 feet. The door would be bolted shut. So there would be no way in or out.

A classic in its own right and perhaps the best match of 1997, The Undertaker's 30-minute contest with Michaels is considered by many to be the best steel cage match in history. It established the new gimmick as a fan favorite. Going into his Hell in a Cell match against the Undertaker, Mick Foley wanted to make his cage bout better than the first.

By mid-summer of 1998, Mick Foley's wrestling career was at its heights. He had faced the biggest babyface in the game, "Stone Cold" Steve Austin, in the WWF's previous two pay-per-view events and was now set to face Austin one last time in Hell in a Cell. But plans changed. "We're just concerned that the audience won't buy another match with you and Steve," a WWF official told Foley over the phone. His "Mankind" persona was just not as "over" as it needed to be to warrant another headline match. So Foley assumed that he was out of the Hell in a Cell bout.

But the official quickly corrected him. "You're still in the Cell. It's just that you'll be in there with the Undertaker."

After a moment of celebration, Foley became concerned. Foley had never wrestled in a cage match in his career, his Mankind character barely registered with fans, and he had faced the Undertaker five times over the last few years on pay-per-view. Their feud had reached a saturation point. Plus, the Undertaker had a broken ankle. Together this seemed like the perfect recipe for a boring contest. "At that point," Foley admitted later, "I had no idea that it would be the most talked-about match of my career."

A couple weeks before the match, Foley and longtime friend, Terry Funk, went to WWF head-quarters in Stamford, Connecticut to view a tape of the Michaels-Undertaker match. "That one is going to be difficult to beat," Funk told Foley. Foley asked his mentor for advice. "I think you ought to start the match on top of the cage," Funk replied after some thought. Later, Funk jokingly suggested that Foley have the Undertaker throw him off the top of the structure. Foley joked along with him: "Then I would climb back up—and he could throw me off again!" Foley mulled over the possibilities and told Terry, "I think I can do it."

He told Mark Callaway, aka The Undertaker, what his plans were. Up until the day before the bout, Callaway refused to comply, despite his trust and respect for Foley after all their years of feuding. "Why are you intent on killing yourself up there?" Callaway asked solemnly. "Because I'm afraid the match is going to stink," he replied. Foley kept chipping away at Callaway, arguing that they had had a wonderful series together and that it would be a shame to ruin it. "I'll think about it," he answered.

On the *King of the Ring* pre-game show that aired one hour before the event, Mankind cut a promo promising fans a special surprise during the pay-per-view. Mick Foley wanted as many viewers as possible to tune in and witness his most daring feat to date.

As Mankind made his way to the ring, the crowd response was minimal. "My entrance received no reaction," Foley remembered. Fan apathy only added fuel to the fire, reminding him why he was about to take the risks he had planned.

At ringside, Mankind paced with his trademark steel chair in hand. His performance was inspired. Unable to settle in one place, Mankind launched the chair airborne on top of the cage.

"What's he doing?" queried color commentator Jerry "The King" Lawler. Mankind grabbed hold and ascended to the top of the cage. "He's supposed to start out inside the cage, isn't he?" a puzzled Lawler continued.

With a deep "BONG" the fans rose to their feet. The house lights dropped. A purple spotlight lit the entranceway, and fans waved lighters as the Undertaker made his spine-chilling entrance. Foley had always admired the Phenom's theatrical ring arrival, but this time it was different. As he paced about awkwardly on top of the cage, Foley could barely retain composure. "Quite frankly," he said, "I was scared as hell now."

"You think he's daring the Undertaker to start the match up there?" Lawler asked. That was the plan. Callaway had at the eleventh hour given his consent to Foley's idea.

As the Undertaker climbed the side of the cage (with his broken ankle), the house lights rose, and the audience popped. Mankind greeted 'Taker with a series of rights, trying to prevent his ascent. With a few rights of his own, 'Taker finally made it on top. "Don't fall on me!" a young fan at ringside could be heard exclaiming.

The chair-wielding madman nailed the Undertaker with several chair-shots to the back. Mankind then gingerly maneuvered his 328-pound foe over to the far side of the cage roof and attempted a suplex. Fans held their breaths—they knew at this point that something big was going to go down.

'Taker blocked the suplex attempt, spun Mankind around with a few meat hook–like blows to the head, grabbed Mankind by the hair and shirt and flung him off the top of the cage!

The awe-struck crowd immediately rose to its feet. "Oh no!" screamed Lawler. "Good God Almighty!" blurted play-by-play man, Jim Ross.

"Suddenly I was airborne—16 feet high and falling fast," Foley recalls.

Mankind crashed through the Spanish announcers' table below. The sound of the table crushing under Foley's 280-pound frame is something no wrestling fan can forget.

"Good God Almighty! They've killed him! As God is my witness, he is broken in half!" Ross shrieked.

"It was the scariest moment of my life, but almost a relief when I landed on the announcer table and felt it crumble beneath my weight," Mankind recollects. "I had missed the monitors on the table, which was my biggest concern, and landed about as perfectly as I could hope for, but the impact had spun me halfway underneath the security railing so that my legs were in the audience."

The roof blew off the Pittsburgh Civic Center! Wrestling fans had never seen, nor would they ever again see, anything quite like this.

"Somebody get out here—really, I mean it," a concerned Ross stated, breaking character.

Mankind lay virtually motionless. "This is over, right here," an equally worried Lawler thought. Had it ended this way, fans would have been satisfied.

The impact of the fall had dislocated Foley's shoulder and left him with a dull pain in his kidney area. Oddly enough, he actually at this moment felt something of an inner peace that the worst was over. "I was about as wrong in that assessment as a human being can possibly be," he later commented.

Several WWF officials, with Terry Funk and an anxious Vince McMahon came out to help Foley. As medical staff wheeled a gurney to ringside, one fan screamed: "Finish the match, man. Do it!"

The packed house rang out with a hockey-like chant, "Un-der-tay-ker," clap, clap, clap. "Apparently as quickly and unusually as this match started, it has ended," explained Ross. The match did indeed look as though it was over as Mankind was being rolled back on the stretcher. But Foley knew otherwise.

Mankind, with his shoulder hanging, rose to his feet and marched back to the cage with a smile on his face. "Look! You've got to be kidding me!" Lawler cried. Fans glared in wonder at this fearless man and rang out with wild cheers. It was only the beginning.

As Mankind amazingly made it back onto the cage, 'Taker hammered him with more rights. The merciless Dead Man then outdid himself. And so did Foley. 'Taker "goozled" Mankind, choke-slammed him and then the cage gave way. Mankind fell through to the ring 12-and-a-half feet down. The crowd went ballistic once again.

"Good God! Good God! Will somebody stop the damn match!" shouted Ross, in a true-to-life appeal for Foley's wellbeing.

It was the first time Mick Foley had ever been legitimately knocked out in his career. For about two minutes, Foley was out cold. Worse, the chair that he had left on top of the cage after the first fall had followed Foley down during the second and smashed into his face. It knocked out one and a half teeth, dislocated his jaw and cut a hole beneath his lip that he could stick his tongue through.

Terry Funk and WWF officials again attended to Foley. Realizing that Foley was out, Funk needed to buy time. As 'Taker jumped through the broken cage roof into the ring, wincing at the pain as he landed on his injured foot, he and Funk began an impromptu exchange that ended when Funk found himself chokeslammed to the mat.

"What happened while I was out was actually a marvel of impromptu ingenuity and a credit to the business," Foley proudly explained. "In a real sport, the action would surely stop if a player was knocked out. But no, we are not a real sport, and no, the action doesn't stop."

Miraculously, Mankind made it to his feet within a few minutes of the devastating fall. The Undertaker sent him back down to the mat with a solid right.

"The scariest moment in the entire match was not either fall, however," Foley later explained, referring to this seemingly harmless right from 'Taker. "When I finally did regain my bearings, there's a moment where the Undertaker punches me, and I did not so much fall as crumble. It represents to me probably the scariest moment of my career, because the lights were on—just barely—but there was nobody home."

Someway, somehow, the match resumed. Mark Callaway didn't think they should continue. "Mick, let's go home," he quietly said to Foley. "No, no, I'm okay," mumbled Foley in reply, lying through what remained of his teeth.

But the man behind the Undertaker was not totally oblivious to Foley's predicament. Without Callaway's poise and experience, the match would clearly have been over. 'Taker bought Foley some more time to recover by allowing him to foil 'Taker's patented walk-the-ropes-forearm move. 'Taker tumbled to the arena floor.

A WWF cameraman then captured one of the most famous images in wrestling history: Mankind sitting in the corner of the ring, smiling, his tongue poking through his punctured lip and a tooth mysteriously dangling from his nostril.

With both men outside the ring, 'Taker grabbed the massive iron steps and slammed them into Mankind's injured shoulder. After a botched suicide dive, in which the Dead Man's skull smacked against the cage—a move that left 'Taker a bloody mess—Mankind mounted an offense. Using the very chair that had made mush of his oral cavity, he piledrove 'Taker's head onto the steel, earning a remarkable near-fall. He then dropped a leg onto 'Taker's face.

"When I landed, I was aware of the terrible pain in my kidney," Foley recalls. "It would actually hurt me for the next eight weeks."

Foley had one more trick up his sleeve. Leaving the ring, he lifted the apron and produced a harmless looking bag. In the ring, its contents would be revealed. Reaching into it, Mankind took a handful of sparkling particles and spread them onto the mat. An already shell-shocked crowd once again rose to its feet, trying to make out what they were. Thumbtacks.

"Ohhhhh!" exclaimed the lively Pittsburgh throng. "My God, this is off the page," Ross asserted.

Mankind emptied 6000 tacks onto the mat. He then locked in his mandible claw hold, hoping to throw an incapacitated 'Taker onto the tacks. The man from Death Valley fought it, picked up Mankind on his back and backed his way toward the area of the ring where the pushpins lay.

"Don't tell me! No!" yelled Ross.

'Taker drilled Mankind back first onto the prickly pad. As Mankind rose to his feet, with hundreds of tacks piercing his flesh and shirt, the Undertaker decided to add insult to injury. "Goozling" Mankind again, 'Taker chokeslammed Mankind hard into the tacks for a second time.

"What else can be done?" Ross shouted. Rising to his feet a human pincushion, Mankind was greeted by the Pittsburgh audience with ringing applause and cheers. 'Taker hooked a bloody and beaten Mankind in the Tombstone piledriver for match-winning three-count.

A genuinely relieved Lawler squealed: "Mercifully, this is over!"

After Undertaker was announced the winner and the crowd gave the match a standing ovation, EMTs appeared and readied the stretcher. Foley refused to leave any other way than on his own two feet.

"How anybody cannot admire the effort of this man, Mankind, Mick Foley, is beyond me," Ross appropriately affirmed. As he walked back to the dressing area, the appreciative crowd, which had greeted him with indifference before the match, chanted, "Foley! Foley! Foley!" Wrestlers backstage met him with the sound of applause as well. Vince McMahon hugged Foley.

Perhaps more astonishing than anything else, Mankind's night wasn't over. An hour or so later, he made a brief run-in during the Kane-Steve Austin main event.

At the end of the night, McMahon walked Foley to his dressing room. "Mick, I want you to know how much we appreciate everything you've done for this company," the WWF owner told Foley. "But please, promise me that you'll never do anything like that ever again."

Reminiscing about the first fall off the top of the cage, Foley estimates that it will be the reason why fans remember him. "With that one move, everything I had accomplished during my 13 years of wrestling became instantly obsolete. For better or worse, that's that one thing I'll be remembered for. I'm proud of it. I'm proud of the fact that we were able to keep on going even after I'd been knocked out."

MAT FACTS

A Work Or Not?

There remains some debate as to whether Mick Foley's second fall through the cage in the Hell in a Cell match was prearranged by Foley and The Undertaker. In his biography, Foley claims that he had no idea that the cage roof would give way. But Foley buddy Terry Funk is on record saying that both falls were scripted. Perhaps we'll never know.

Prickly Subject

Mick Foley claims to have been the first wrestler to use thumbtacks in a wrestling match. It was in 1995, he argues, that he introduced them into the squared circle. While this may be the case, he was not the innovator of the Thumbtacks Match. The IWA Japan promotion, for which Foley wrestled in the same year in the now infamous King of the Death Match tournament, was the first promotion to stage a Thumbtacks Match. Officials place a tray in the middle of the ring, and thousands of thumbtacks are poured into it. During IWA Japan's Kawasaki Dream card on August 20, 1995, Shoji Nakamaki fought former tag team partner, Hiroshi, and powerbombed him onto the thumbtacks.

Big Japan Pro Wrestling staged a Thumbtacks In Balloons match on March 22, 1996. The match that saw Axl Rotten and Shoji Nakamaki lock up with Kendo Nagasaki and Seiji Yamakawa had six black balloons suspended above the ring. At a certain point in the match, the balloons exploded and released 30,000 thumbtacks onto the competitors.

Cage-O-Rama

There have been 14 Hell in a Cell bouts in WWF/WWE history, but the history of the cage bout reaches far back into wrestling history. The first cage match took place on July 2, 1937, in Atlanta, Georgia between Jack Bloomfield and Count Petro Rossi. For this contest, the ring was surrounded by chicken wire in order to keep the athletes inside and fend off any outside interference from other wrestlers. While little is known about this match, it does seem to be the earliest form of a steel cage match in recorded history. Others credit late promoter Paul Boesch with the idea of the steel cage match. The roots of the cage match in Texas lie in Galveston, where officials wrapped a ring in fishing net for a match between the hardcore Wild Bull Curry and Dirty Don Evans. The concept was not well received, but the idea did pave the way for something more attractive: the fence match. The fence match predates the steel cage match but was similar in style and execution to the cage matches seen in later years.

The classic steel cage match might also be traced back to Los Angeles, California, and the famous Grand Olympic Auditorium. In the late 1960s, Freddie Blassie, with promoter Mike LeBell, created and promoted the Blassie Cage to blow off his feuds with wrestlers like John Tolos and The Sheik. While most cage matches end on a pinfall or submission, these Blassie Cage matches ended with one wrestler escaping over the top of the cage or exiting through the door. Some say that it was the brainchild of Fred Blassie himself.

The WWF introduced its thick, grid-like cage as part of a storyline between Hulk Hogan and King Kong Bundy leading into *WrestleMania 2*. The Federation used the cage until 1999 when they switched to chain link because it had more give. Since then, the grid-like cage has only been used twice, for Edge vs. Christian at *Rebellion 2001* and for the Al Snow vs. Big Boss Man at *Unforgiven 1999*.

WWE has also experimented with other types of cages, including the Hell in a Cell and the multi-competitor Elimination Chamber.

Variations of the steel cage match in the NWA/WCW include a special barbed wire–topped steel cage created by Ric Flair, the Thundercage (roofless, its walls curved inward), the WarGames Cage, the Triple Cage (a gigantic three-tiered structure that was essentially a Hell In A Cell cage with a standard roofed cage on top, with a third smaller cage on top of that) and the grid-like bar cage used for Hulk Hogan vs. "Rowdy" Roddy Piper at *Halloween Havoc '97*.

Chapter Seven

A Tribute Gripped By Tragedy

Kansas City was as important as any night I ever had in my life, let alone wrestling.

–Bret "The Hitman" Hart

Former seven-time NWA world champion Harley Race, a legendary sports figure in the Kansas City area, was present at the October 4, 1999, edition of *WCW Monday Nitro* to make the ring introductions. "I'm here to introduce a match that, of all the accolades that have been thrown at me in my career, this right here probably means more than 99.9 percent of them." Out from behind the curtain came a teary-eyed Chris Benoit pounding his chest as a symbol of respect. He gave Harley Race a hug in the center of the ring. The Kansas City crowd applauded respectfully. Benoit was followed by Hart, who bit his lip as he courageously walked the aisle past the thousands of people in attendance. While Bret took his turn hugging and thanking Race for his appearance, even WCW referee Mickey Jay took an emotionally charged deep breath.

Rarely does it happen, but both competitors in this contest embraced each other before the bout as well.

A fan at ringside lifted up his placard proudly. "We miss you Owen," it read. The thousands in attendance joined together in a polite chant of "O-wen, O-wen, O-wen." Bret allowed himself a modest smile in response. On the surface, he had his game face on. Under the surface was a well of emotions.

WCW announcer Mike Tenay read off a statement from Bret for the benefit of the television audience as the opening bell rang: "By far this will be the single most important time that I've ever stepped into the ring. I'll try to do my brother proud. I hope my best is good enough. I dedicate this match to Owen Hart and to those who loved him."

Bret Hart's match with Chris Benoit sticks in our memories because of his brother Owen's death in that same arena six months earlier.

On May 23, 1999, in the middle of the WWF's *Over the Edge* supercard, an emotional Jim Ross, the WWF's lead announcer, had had the unenviable task of making the following announcement to a live pay-per-view audience: "Owen Hart was set to make an entrance from the ceiling, and he fell from the ceiling. I have the unfortunate responsibility to let everyone know that Owen Hart has died. Owen Hart has tragically died from that accident here tonight." Ross's longtime broadcast partner, Jerry "The King" Lawler, also shown on camera during this statement, quite visibly had difficulty holding the tears back. It was a tragic death—a heavy blow for the entire wrestling world and especially the Hart family.

The story is by now well known. The 34-year-old Owen Hart, who had recently reprised his buffoonish superhero "Blue Blazer" gimmick, was set to be lowered to the ring from the rafters for his contest. While being lowered, the harness carrying Hart's 227 pounds gave way, sending him crashing to the mat 78-feet below. Reports have it that Owen's chest hit one of the corner turnbuckles, propelling him into the ring. His aorta was severed upon impact, and his lungs filled with blood. Owen was pronounced dead less than an hour later. The crowd at the Kemper Arena in Kansas City, Kansas, witnessed the tragedy live. The pay-per-view audience was watching a video package during Owen's fall and was thankfully spared the spectacle.

The next night, the WWF presented a special edition of *Raw Is War*, entitled "Raw Is Owen," in which wrestlers and personnel were invited to cut interviews sharing their memories of Owen and prayers for his family. The touching tribute show captured the hearts and minds of wrestling and non-wrestling TV viewers alike. The show garnered the highest rating ever for a Monday night cable wrestling broadcast.

At that time, Bret Hart, Owen's older brother, was wrestling with the WWF's competition, World Championship Wrestling. He had, of course, been "screwed" by WWF owner Vince McMahon at the *Survivor Series* in 1997 held in Montreal, Quebec. Despite leaving the company on the worst of terms, years after his brother's accident Bret Hart couldn't help but express that he wished he had been working for the WWF at the time of the incident.

"I don't beat myself over the head with it, but I've always wished that I had been with the WWF when Owen's accident happened," commented a remorseful Bret. "I've always felt a deep sense of loss and agonized over what brought about the fact that I wasn't there to always be there for him like I had been for so many years. Looking over his shoulder." Had he been there, Bret might have been able to talk Owen out of accepting the risks that went along with such an over-the-top ring entrance. Or, he might have been there to double-check that the harness was solid, safe. But none of this was meant to be.

Owen's death tore down the curtain separating the two wrestling promotions. And it remains one of the few occasions during the heated WCW-WWF Monday Night Wars of 1995–2001 that events unfolding in one directly affected the programming of the other.

Thirteen days after *Over the Edge,* Bret appeared on *WCW Monday Nitro*—his first appearance after Owen's death—to deliver a touching promo. "On behalf of my whole family and everybody back in Calgary, we want to thank all the wrestling fans all around the world that have sent their love and their support and their condolences," Bret told the thousands in attendance and the millions watching at home. "There are a lot of fans and wrestlers that got to know him, and I don't think that there's anybody that could say a bad thing about him anywhere. He was my closest brother. We were close from the time he was in diapers. And I take a lot of pride in knowing how well he had turned out."

It was a period of reflection for committed Owen Hart fans as well. He was the consummate professional, reliable, unassuming and entertaining. Even the casual fan could see this. Owen brought to wrestling fans a number of classic moments that will not soon be forgotten. His hard-fought

WrestleMania V technical battle with WWE Hall of Famer "Mr. Perfect" Curt Hennig and the spectacular back flip he executed every time he entered the ring stood out. So did his classic, 20-minute belter at *WrestleMania X* against his own brother Bret, where he scored his first high-profile victory in North America. There was also his scorching *SummerSlam '94* steel cage loss to Bret, his hard-fought 1997 loss to the late "British Bulldog" in the finals of a new WWF European championship in Berlin, his impressive battle with Vader at WWF's first UK pay-per-view, *One Night Only* and his hilarious week-to-week performance as the whiny, meddling, double-Slammy-Award–winning member of the Hart Foundation in 1997.

When WCW decided to return to Kemper Arena for the first time since Owen's death with a live broadcast of *Monday Nitro* in October 1999, Bret wanted to do something special to commemorate his brother. It was a time when both *Nitro* and *Raw* were at the height of the Crash TV era, cramming segments with bikini contests, lengthy promos, "This is your life" presentations and pull-apart brawls. In this "anything-but-wrestling" era, Bret wanted to express his love for his brother with a traditional match. He wanted to wrestle. WCW officials immediately agreed.

But who would Bret choose as his opponent?

He chose a man who knew the Hart Family so well that Bret considered him a member of the clan. He had been trained in Stu Hart's infamous "Dungeon" facility in the Hart Family basement in Calgary, Alberta: the "Rabid Wolverine," Chris Benoit. He was a wrestler in the Hart mold—a no-nonsense technician dedicated to the craft of wrestling.

Benoit, perhaps more than any other wrestler, dedicated his life to professional wrestling. He was respected and admired by fans and colleagues alike. Fans famously expressed gratitude for his gritty, never-say-die perseverance and commitment to the sport with a standing ovation for his losing efforts in an outstanding WWE championship match against Kurt Angle at the *2003 Royal Rumble*. Many shed tears of elation when he captured the world title in the main event of *WrestleMania XX,* culminating his 19-year struggle to ascend to the pinnacle of the industry. As the capacity crowd at Madison Square Garden and the then record-setting pay-per-view audience cheered, Benoit greeted the WWE champion Eddie Guerrerro in the ring with an emotional embrace. It was a moment for the ages. Readers of *Pro Wrestling Illustrated* voted Benoit's victory over HHH and Shawn Michaels as the 2004 Match of the Year.

Bret's respect for Benoit both as a man and as a wrestler in the days and weeks leading up to the Owen tribute match on *Nitro* was unequivocal.

He actually wanted to lose to him in the tribute match! But WCW management felt that it would be more fitting for Bret to come out on top.

From the opening bell, The Hitman and The Crippler didn't hold back. They began the match slowly, exchanging headlocks and armlocks. Several minutes into the bout, they let loose with higher impact blows—chops, forearm shots, a DDT. Bret made a flying elbow drop from the middle rope.

Hart, ever the tactician, began to zero in on Benoit's back, executing a hard backbreaker and, outside the ring, slamming The Crippler's spine against the ring apron. But Benoit upped the ante. The crowd popped as Benoit flipped over to avoid another Hitman backbreaker and sent Bret cranium-first to the canvas with a picture-perfect tombstone piledriver. Benoit earned a close two-count. Those in attendance, more and more behind Bret as the match unfolded, applauded in relief as Hart's shoulder came up.

Leaping into the air, Benoit hoped to catch Hart with a flying dropkick. Instead, Hart held onto the ropes as Benoit fell back first to the mat. The Hitman took over with a crisp belly-to-back suplex. Hart now earned a close near-fall. Sticking Benoit up against the ropes and peppering Benoit with several hard rights, Hart bounced off the opposite ropes and charged toward his opponent.

Down but not out, Benoit moved, and The Hitman sprung back from the ropes and crashed to the mat.

After Hart rolled out to the floor, Benoit exploded through the top and middle ropes with a suicide dive, connecting head-to-head with Hart, who was propelled backward 10 feet up the aisle. Both men were hurt.

This seesaw, methodical battle raged on as Hart once again gained control, resuming his attack on Benoit's back. Like a piece of dynamite with a short fuse, Benoit quickly exploded with a roll-up or a backslide or a small package as he tried to chip away at Hart's advantage. But The Hitman continued the assault.

Crotching Benoit on the top turnbuckle, Hart ascended to the top strand and lifted the Rabid Wolverine over with a devastating superplex. Both wrestlers lay in agony on the mat. One could feel the atmosphere in the Kemper Arena build in anticipation for the match's conclusion.

The Hitman battled to his feet first, grabbing hold of Benoit's legs. He was going for his patented Sharpshooter leglock. Benoit, a master of counterholds, clasped Hart's left arm and hooked in his patented submission hold, the Crippler Crossface.

As the crowd roared for him, Bret Hart knew that he had to dig down deep. Benoit wrenched back on his neck, but Bret had to battle out of the hold—for Owen.

As he fought his way to the ropes and the crowd responded positively, Hart winced in pain. Benoit snapped Bret over with three solid suplexes. He then flew gracefully through the air, nailing Hart with a beautiful flying headbutt. Benoit covered Hart. One…Two…NO! The Calgary native kicked out. He still had fight left in him!

A "Let's go Bret! Let's go Bret!" chant filled the arena.

The tide turned. Hart blasted Benoit with a terrific piledriver of his own. But he couldn't hold Benoit down for the count.

Going hold-for-hold, Benoit tried three German suplexes. Hart resisted the third, unleashing a series of clubbing blows to Benoit's weakened back. Hooking Benoit for a vertical suplex, Benoit instinctively clasped Bret's arm, hoping to once again lock in the Crossface. Simultaneously, The Hitman grabbed hold of The Crippler's leg, hoping that he could hook his tenacious foe in the Sharpshooter. As the wrestlers pulled and wrenched at one another, the fans knew that they were watching two of the very best at their very best.

Hart outwrestled Benoit, pulling his arm free just long enough to maneuver Benoit around, grapevine his legs and twist him over into Hart's excruciating Sharpshooter. Fans arose out of their seats. Would Benoit fight out of it?

Hart's ring positioning was perfect—Benoit had nowhere to go. Less than 10 seconds after falling victim to the hold, Benoit gave up.

The respectful Kansas City fans, some of whom had witnessed Owen's deadly fall first hand, erupted in appreciation. Not only for Bret Hart's win. They recognized the masterful wrestling these two grapplers had put on display in commemoration of Owen Hart.

Bret, his hand raised in victory, looked up at the rafters from which Owen had fallen and saluted. Bret and Chris then embraced in the center of the ring. Referee Mickey Jay led the crowd in a round of applause.

"Kansas City was as important as any night I ever had in my life, let alone wrestling," commented a contemplative Bret. "I really felt that Owen was right there, above the ring watching. And in a lot of ways it was a match for one person. There was one person in the audience."

Bret Hart would retire in 2000 after sustaining a debilitating concussion, but on this night in Kansas City, he had put together one of the great matches of his illustrious 24-year career. Rarely has the sport of professional wrestling—so often marred by adolescent antics and obscene, lowbrow storylines—been more worthy of respect than during this admirable tribute match.

If we remember Bret's work that evening proudly, we remember the image of Benoit standing in the ring hugging Bret after the tribute match very differently. Despite his professional accomplishments and the respect he deserves for his wrestling during this important match, his reputation is hounded by the mysterious final hours of his life in June 2007, Benoit sedated and murdered his seven-year-old son Daniel and his wife Nancy before taking his own life.

The timeline of events from that tragic weekend in 2007 are still fresh in many fans' minds. On Saturday, June 23, Benoit was scheduled to appear at a *Smackdown* house show in Beaumont, Texas. He missed his flight and left an unnamed coworker a cryptic voicemail: "I love you." Later the same day, he called this and another coworker explaining that his wife and son had been sick with food poisoning. On Sunday, June 24, between 3:53 and 3:58 AM, five bizarre text messages were sent from the cell phones of Benoit and his wife. The messages either repeated his exact home address or else explained that the dogs Benoit owned were in the enclosed pool area and the garage door was open. The coworkers didn't know what to make of the messages and dismissed them. The WWE made several attempts to contact the

Benoits to no avail. Midday Monday, WWE management, after learning about the text messages, contacted the local sheriff's office and requested that they make a welfare call to Benoit's residence. At 4:00 PM on June 25, the three bodies were found in their home.

Only days after the tragic events, a perplexed former WWE star and fellow Canadian Chris Jericho told Fox News that "the guy that I knew and I loved was a loving, polite, good, friendly, heartfelt, genuine man, someone I looked up to and always emulated and viewed as an inspiration." He explained further: "that's why it is so hard to come up with some semblance or shred of reason explaining why he could snap. What caused this man who was so mild-mannered and such a good man and such a loving father, a loving friend, a loving husband to snap in this way and commit these violent acts? I don't think we'll ever know."

Should the ghastly double murder-suicide tarnish Benoit's legacy as a wrestler? For now, it's too early to tell if his in-ring accomplishments will be overshadowed by his inexplicably grisly end. But for his part, Bret Hart had no doubt that there was some good inside the man who stepped up and helped him offer a fitting tribute to his dead brother. As he tersely explained to CTV NewsNet, "What happened was not by the Chris Benoit I knew."

MAT FACTS

Toothless Aggression?

Benoit, famously missing one tooth, did not actually lose it while training or during a wrestling match. One day, Benoit was struck beneath the chin by his pet Rottweiler's head while play wrestling with the dog, and his tooth just popped out.

A Thousand Holds Minus One

The "Man of a Thousand Holds" Dean Malenko has actually been credited by Chris Benoit with teaching him the Crippler Crossface.

Mysteries of the Harness

For weeks after Owen's tragic fall, there was a great deal of discussion about the harness he used that night, especially on the quick-release trigger and safety latches. When someone is lowered from the rafters in a harness, there are backup latches that must be latched for safety purposes. These backups may take some time to unlatch, which would have made Owen's stunt difficult to perform smoothly. Therefore, it was apparently decided the safety backups would not be used, allowing Owen to unlatch himself more quickly.

A further problem was that the harness Owen used was designed for sailboats and required only six pounds of weight to trigger the quick-release mechanism. Owen weighed about 225 pounds.

An out-of-court settlement between Owen Hart's family and the WWF has prevented the release of any information about the harness.

A Young Family

Owen Hart left behind a widow, Martha and two children, Oje Edward and Athena.

OH

At Owen's funeral, there was a WWF logo made entirely out of yellow flowers. Martha Hart requested that it be removed and replaced with Owen's initials.

Legal Tender

Following Owen's death, Martha Hart settled a wrongful death lawsuit against the WWF out-of-court for approximately $18 million and used the funds to establish the Owen Hart Foundation, which she has managed since 1999. In 2002, Martha published a book about Owen's life, *Broken Harts: The Life and Death of Owen Hart.*

More Tributes

ECW performed a tribute to Owen after his death by having all talent come to the ring while the bell tolled 34 times (Owen was 34 at the time of his death). Moreover, the video game *WWF Attitude* on the Nintendo 64 and Sony PlayStation was dedicated to Hart's memory.

A Canadian Tradition

In 1988, Owen Hart wrestled for New Japan Pro Wrestling (NJPW) on several tours. On May 27, he defeated Hiroshi Hase for the IWGP Junior Heavyweight Championship. Owen became the first westerner to hold that coveted title, one which would be won by Chris Benoit two years later.

Chapter Eight

Glory Bound?

I'll believe it's not gonna last when I see it.
                                        –A.J. Styles

Allen Lloyd Jones is better known to wrestling fans as "The Phenomenal" A.J. Styles. He once competed in the WCW under the name of "Air Styles" as one half of the tag team, Air Raid. For a 22-year-old who had been in wrestling for just over two years, it was a big break to appear on nationally televised WCW wrestling events in buildings that would attract thousands of fans. Unfortunately, his big break was too good to last. In the spring of 2001, WCW, the promotion that had nearly run the WWE out of business in the mid-'90s, went belly up. Suddenly, Styles and many other WCW stars found themselves in the unemployment line.

WWE Hall of Famer Eddie Guerrerro remembered the uncertainty of that time clearly. He had left WCW to wrestle for the WWE in early 2000, but his nephew, Chavo Guerrerro, had remained with the now defunct promotion. "I felt concern for my nephew Chavo—and not only Chavo, but a lot of the boys" he said.

WCW's problem was bad management. The company was losing an astonishing $15 million per year. Officials tried to bring in former WCW president Eric Bischoff, who had been fired in late 1999, to restore order. During his tenure, he had taken WCW, a Southern-based regional company that was losing $10 million per year and transformed it into a multinational corporation that was earned $350 million per year in sales and $40 million in profit. He was also the only man to give Vince McMahon a run for his money, winning 83 straight ratings victories in head-to-head competition over the WWF. But rather than coming back to manage the company, he tried unsuccessfully to buy it from Time Warner. Unfortunately, he was unable to finalize the deal, and the company was forced to close its doors.

Ric Flair, who remained with WCW to the last and competed against longtime rival Sting on the final episode of *Monday Nitro,* which aired on March 26, 2001, was especially upset. "I was so happy at that last show to see that company close down, I couldn't stand it. I couldn't wait for the curtain to go down." He was angry over the mismanagement that had caused the once dominant promotion to crumble. But he had mixed feelings too. "I was sad at the same time to see all these people who were losing their jobs, who had nowhere to go."

Over at the WWE, owner Vince McMahon stepped in, purchased WCW's video library, trademarks and some talent contracts for $4.3 million. Many longtime WWE employees gloated as if they'd scored a victory in the ring. WWE official Gerald Brisco proudly proclaimed: "This was probably the defining moment, when we finally conquered WCW owner Ted Turner and all his billions and billions of dollars and told Ted, 'We kicked your butt!'"

Styles, one of the many casualties of the WCW-WWE war, returned to NWA Wildside, an independent wrestling promotion based out of Atlanta, Georgia, where he had wrestled in his rookie year. The crowds were smaller, peaking at 175 diehards, shows were broadcast on local television stations in late-night timeslots, and the pay was considerably less. It was a quite a setback, and his career prospects were down the tubes.

Yet Styles was confident that he had enough talent and desire to wrestle in front of bright lights and large crowds. "I was definitely back to square one when WCW went out of business," Styles remembers. "It took a toll on me. I was depressed for a week or two. But I worked my way back up. I still had high hopes for A.J. Styles."

On October 13, 2001, Styles wrestled on the NWA's 53rd Anniversary show. His opponent—independent wrestling star Christopher Daniels. Daniels, known as "The King of Indies" among industry insiders because of his work on independent shows around the world, was also employed by WCW at the time of the company's collapse.

Styles and Daniels competed in the match of the night. Some fans even call their high-flying display the match of the year. This was first time these two grinders ever met, both in the ring and out. Little did they know, especially in this tumultuous period in the American wrestling industry, that their futures would be bright and that their fortunes would be intertwined.

The Atlanta-based World Championship Wrestling wasn't the only major wresting promoter to go under in the spring of 2001, and Styles and his WCW cohorts weren't the only wrestlers looking for steady work. The Philadelphia-based Extreme Championship Wrestling went under at the same time as WCW. In fact, a major British wrestling magazine that announced the WWE was buying WCW also ran a lead story in the same issue head-lined "Goodbye ECW." Wrestling analysts and

Internet dirt sheets scrambled to make sense of the simultaneous demise of North America's number two and number three wrestling organizations.

About six months before its collapse, ECW officials received some bad news. In October 2000, cable network TNN (The National Network, now Spike TV) announced that it had cancelled ECW's flagship show, *ECW on TNN*, which at the time was the network's highest rated broadcast. ECW had lost its time slot after the network acquired WWE programming, putting the company in jeopardy. "We're DEAD, and we can't get out of the line of fire," exclaimed ECW owner Paul Heyman some-time later, giving his take on of the effects of TNN's notorious refusal to allow ECW to negotiate with another network while it signed a deal with WWE. After being kicked to the curb and losing its TV deal, ECW scraped along until Heyman finally declared bankruptcy on April 4, 2001.

"It was a horrible time," mumbled ECW Original, Tommy Dreamer, reflecting on ECW's last days. Many wrestlers were in denial about the company's fate and their own, and those that weren't were worried about how they were going to put food on the table for their young families.

ECW's last world champion, the "Man Beast" Rhino, was perhaps hit hardest by the news. "I didn't think ECW was going to fold," he confessed. On the night of the last ECW show, Rhino refused to join the rest of the company's remaining talent in the ring for the final goodbye. "I wouldn't go out there because I believed in my heart it wasn't over," he continued as his eyes welled up. "I remember looking on the ECW website to see if there were any dates announced. I didn't want it to end. I was somebody. I felt like somebody. I was definitely in denial for a couple of years after it closed."

"There were lots of guys that were just not going to have anywhere else to go," commented ECW's breakout star, Rob Van Dam, who had high hopes that he'd eventually find a spot in WWE.

"All of a sudden, the next thing I knew, I was out of a job," remembers ECW stalwart, Nunzio, who would luckily find employment in WWE. With both the ECW and the WCW closing within a month of each other, there were suddenly "90 wrestlers on the market, and you've only got WWE there."

Throughout the summer and fall of 2001, a select few of ECW's talent found jobs with the WWE. But most were forced to either leave the wrestling industry or ply their trade in the minor leagues as A.J. Styles had done.

Back in the NWA-Wildside, Styles' unemployment worries diminished, and his career as an independent exploded despite the odds. In the wake of the 53rd Anniversary show's success, he was accepting bookings on cards from coast to coast in the U.S. In April 2002, he flew to Australia to wrestle for the short-lived World Wrestling All-Stars (WWA) promotion. There, he was reunited with some other former WCW stars, who had also been eking out a living on independent shows. Among them was former four-time WCW world title-holder, Jeff Jarrett.

"I'm thinking of launching a promotion of my own," Jarrett told Styles. Jarrett had a vision. He knew that there were enough talented stars on the independent market to give the WWE a run for its money on the national level.

Despite his success, Styles knew that wrestling on small, independent cards was only a short-term solution. He wanted a more stable employment and had high hopes for the Jarrett-led league. "I was just praying that this company would start up," admitted Styles. "You'd keep hearing rumors at this time of new companies starting up. I just prayed that this one would and hire A.J. Styles." He was not the only one praying.

Not long thereafter, Jarrett and his father, veteran promoter Jerry, announced the launch of NWA: TNA (Total Nonstop Action). Although Styles was hoping to be a part of TNA's inaugural show, he had yet to hear from the Jarretts. Around the same time, Styles was approached by WWE and offered a developmental deal. Obsessed with superstardom, The Phenomenal One had an important decision to make. Should he accept the WWE's offer or hold out in hopes that TNA would come calling? Which of the two options would be best for his career—and his family?

"The WWE's deal wasn't very good," comments a candid Styles. "I was offered $500 a week to move to Cincinnati." The WWE wanted to groom Styles' in-ring technique at its affiliate Heartland Wrestling Association (HWA) before giving him the chance to compete on the national stage. He was split. The problem was that Styles' wife was still in college at the time, chasing her dream of becoming a schoolteacher. This meant that if Styles accepted the WWE's offer, then he could no longer support his academically inclined wife. She would have to move back in with her parents and put pressure on them for financial support. Styles declined WWE's risky offer.

Two weeks later, TNA came calling, just as he had hoped. But TNA's debut show, not to mention its first couple of months, was rough going for Styles and the upstart organization.

TNA officials hoped that fans would embrace their product as a viable alternative to the WWE from the get-go. But because it had yet to secure a television deal and desperately needed to draw revenue to sustain itself on a weekly basis, TNA's initial programming consisted of a two-hour pay-per-view every Wednesday night for $9.95. This approach and other difficulties hampered TNA's popularity with fans from the start.

But TNA did have some early successes. A cornerstone of TNA cards was a new concept: the X Division. A variant on the WCW and WWE cruiserweight divisions, which had in turn come out of ECW's earlier successes booking junior heavyweight matches, the X Division would feature a high-risk, high-energy wrestling style. Lighter wrestlers around the world applauded the creation of the division. The WWE had notoriously been "the land of the giants," and cruiserweights were never given the chance to show off their creative acrobatics when they competed in front of WWE fans. But the new X Division wasn't about protecting leaner, smaller competitors and, in fact, had no upper weight limit.

In order to capture the essence of this innovative division, TNA announcer Mike Tenay coined this slogan: "It's not about weight limits; it's about no limits." TNA had developed a concept that would immediately distinguish its product from that of the WWE.

"The first show that TNA ever had in Huntsville, Alabama, on June 19, 2002, I was terrified," remembers Styles. "Right as we were about to go live, the ring broke down—big time." The TNA ring crew managed to repair it, but this left Styles—a high flyer who relied heavily on the

top strand for his daredevil maneuvers—uneasy.
A broken top rope would severely inhibit the match.
Styles' goal of leaving a lasting impression with TNA
fans from the start was at risk. "X Division wrestlers
need to go out there and tear it up. Everybody was
praying! People I didn't even know who prayed
were praying!" A lot of young wrestlers had high
hopes for their futures in TNA. What a shame it
would be if a defective ring cost the promotion its
chance!

The ring survived, Styles competed in a tremendous six-man match with cruiserweights Low Ki
and Jerry Lynn, among others. The healthy crowd
of 3000 appeared satisfiedwith the show, and TNA
limped along.

From a creative standpoint, the company lacked
direction, and the product was a mixture of very
good and positively dire in-ring action. The first
show featured hungry up-and-comers like
Styles. But there were also midget matches, a tag
team named The Johnsons (who dressed up like
phalluses) and a lingerie Battle Royal in which
announcer Ed Ferrara groped a female competitor's
breasts. Hard-hitting, athletic action and these
Crash TV elements mixed like oil and water.
Worse, TNA brought in WWE mid-card talent for
which the WWE could largely find no use like
former UFC notable Ken Shamrock, the booze-
sodden Scott Hall, high-guy Brian Christopher and

the arrogant Buff Bagwell. This gave TNA the feel of a cut-rate, low-budget WWE.

By July, the Jarretts were losing $120,000 per week. Company morale was at an all-time low. Pay-per-view buy rates and attendance were poor. Following the August 21, 2002, show, it was announced that there were no further plans to produce live pay-per-views for the foreseeable future. Most wrestling pundits saw this as the end for the company. TNA's bid to become North America's number two organization looked like it was over.

But TNA returned on September 18, and then in October, the Jarretts were saved from extinction. A multimillion-dollar company called Panda Energy invested substantially in the Jarretts' operation. With Panda's resources behind it, TNA could finally pour real money into the development of its image and roster.

"Did I think TNA was going to make it?" Styles thinks back. "No, nobody did. It almost didn't several times. Somehow we kept on."

After months of baffling, uninspired and even tasteless storylines and matches, the product finally began to come together. TNA dropped the Crash TV horseplay and emphasized thrilling X Division performers like Styles, Low Ki, Jerry Lynn and one of Styles' old friends, Christopher Daniels. The league also began to focus attention on Jeff Jarrett's newly won NWA world title. TNA had found an identity.

In January 2003, TNA fans were abuzz over the first headline-grabbing jump of a WWE wrestler to TNA: former two-time ECW world champion Raven. One thousand fans packed the Nashville Fairgrounds (now nicknamed the TNA Asylum) for a gripping NWA world title match on April 30 that saw Jarrett successfully defend against his gothic foe.

Around this time, Styles, whom many considered TNA's best worker and who had wrestled in a number of cracking X Division battles in the preceding months, was approached by TNA officials about winning the NWA world title. Although he had won both the X Division and Tag Team titles in TNA, this would give Styles a shot at being this company's franchise player. Styles remembers the moment fondly: "Here's the thing. They're saying that A.J. Styles as NWA champion is the guy that's going to put butts in the seats. If they're going to say that, what an honor for them even to put the belt on me. To me, it is the most recognized belt in the world. Everybody knows about the NWA title."

That Styles would be elevated to such a level at the age of 26 and on the eve of TNA's anniversary celebration was a shocker to many. Many fans doubted that the 215-pound Georgia native could carry himself as the company's top man—both in the ring and out.

Snubbing the naysayers, a rule-breaking Styles defeated Jarrett and Raven in a Triple Threat match for the NWA world title on June 4, 2003. Styles became the company's first Triple-Crown titleholder, having held all three of the league's major titles. During his four-month reign, he also grew into his role as a conceited heel champion, defending the title in superb matches against Raven and former partner D-Lo Brown. He even squeezed a decent contest out of 58-year old former three-time NWA champ, Dusty Rhodes. Styles showed many that he could make it as world champion.

Styles would lose the title back to Jarrett on October 22, but his career was rolling and so was TNA. He would win world titles again in 2004 and 2005 as the company grew, found a stable and loyal audience and signed free agents like former WCW stars Sting and Kevin Nash and WWE defectors Team 3-D (formerly the Dudley Boys) and Christian Cage. TNA was becoming healthier, and stars like Styles started to shine as the competition stiffened.

But the highlight of Style's young career was yet to come.

Among the new talent TNA was able to acquire in this period was the 290-pound independent star

Samoa Joe. The hard-hitting "Samoan Submission Machine" was courted on behalf of TNA by Christopher Daniels. Joe respected Daniels for the years he had toughed it out on the independent circuit. But, like Styles before him, Joe was also entertaining offers from WWE. Since WWE would not have been the best home for his stiff wrestling style, Joe leaned towards TNA, knowing that TNA would give him a shot at superstardom in front of a national audience without asking him to tone down his aggressive matches. He wanted to be his own man.

He wasted no time proving himself.

After signing with TNA on June 14, 2005, and debuting on its *Slammiversary 2005* pay-per-view show five days later, Joe immediately lobbied to wrestle in what he perceived to be the division that best suited his style and his wish to make an immediate impact: the X Division. Joe faced Styles in the final of the Christopher Daniels Invitational X-Cup tournament at TNA's *Sacrifice* event on August 15. He made Styles tap out to the "Coquina Clutch" rear naked choke to earn a shot at "The Fallen Angel" Christopher Daniel's X Division Title at TNA's next major event, *Unbreakable*. And he managed this, despite Daniels' outside interference in the match. As a result of the interference, TNA officials made the match a Three-Way Dance between Styles, Daniels and Samoa Joe for the now-prestigious X Division championship.

Little did the TNA fans that filled the aptly named Impact! Zone in Orlando, Florida, know that they were about to witness the greatest match in TNA history.

It was the daredevil risk takers Styles and Daniels matched up with the heavy-hitting, undefeated mat specialist Joe. It was the "Styles Clash" inverted mat slam versus the "Angel's Wings" spinning double under-hook facebuster versus the "Coquina Clutch."

Fittingly, TNA officials decided to make the match the main event of one of their most important shows of the year. It even followed the NWA championship match.

While these three hungry young athletes had competed against each other before in one-on-one battles, this match had a special feel from the beginning. A big match atmosphere filled the small arena and revved up the rabid wrestling fans. The first wrestler to earn a pinfall or submission would be the winner.

The 26–year-old Joe, with a staid look on his face, made his way to the ring first to rousing chants of "Joe! Joe! Joe!" Styles then emerged from the entranceway, throwing off his trademark hoodie. "This is my time," he shouted to the pumped throng.

"There's nothing he hasn't accomplished in TNA," confirmed commentator Don West. "But this could be his toughest battle yet."

Finally, "The Fallen Angel"—a 33-year-old, 12-year pro who had held the X Division title for a record 182 days—entered the arena. He calmly walked the ring apron, tore his gothic-style hood from his bald cranium and stared straight at the television camera. "This will be my finest hour!" he screamed. How true those words would prove to be.

The referee called for the bell. Daniels immediately began taunting his two foes—"This is my belt! I'm Mr. TNA!" Joe and Styles stormed the cocky champion with a series of beat-down blows. The two challengers double-teamed the champion with a series of chops and stiff kicks to the back. Styles and Joe tried to outdo one another in a game of one-upmanship. Feeling an adrenaline rush, Daniels hopped to his feet and was greeted with two more kicks that sent him back to the mat. The crowd applauded the action.

Their temporary pact broken, Joe and Styles exchanged roll-ups and submission holds. Daniels—down but not out—joined the fray, catching Styles with a stiff leg lariat. The action in the first few minutes of the bout was hard and fast.

While holding Styles in a headlock, Daniels stormed Joe with an *insiguri* head kick and followed through with a bulldog on Styles. Unable to capture the three-count on Styles, Daniels attempted the combo once again, only to find himself thrown off by Styles and aggressively spike-slammed by Joe.

In these early stages of the bout, none of the competitors could gain the advantage. Styles dominated Joe briefly but was quickly thrown in a belly-to-belly overhead suplex into the turnbuckles. Fans continued to applaud every move.

Not to be outdone, Daniels shoulder-blocked Joe outside the ring and threw caution to the wind, catching his stunned foe with a split-legged springboard moonsault onto the arena floor. This was only the first in a series of daredevil moves to come!

Fans roared, "TNA! TNA! TNA!"

"They know that they're seeing three of the best wrestlers in the world vying for one of the most significant titles," West pointed out.

Styles saw an opening. As Joe and Daniels brawled at ringside, Style took to the air with a tremendous shooting star press from the top rope to the arena floor. "Did you see the gracefulness?

Did you see the style?" screamed West. The audience rang out with a chant that is music to a professional wrestler's ears.

Clutching his mid-section, Styles rolled Joe into the ring for a near-fall. The pace then quickened. Following a leapfrog, Styles caught Joe with a drop-kick to the chin. Styles earned another two-count.

But in a three-way match, one has to have eyes in the back of one's head. Daniels forearmed Styles from behind and whipped him into the opposite corner. Joe then hammered Daniels and fired him in Styles' direction. Daniels leaped onto Styles and monkey-flipped Styles onto Joe. Amazingly, Styles caught Joe in a head scissors and took Joe the mat with a scintillating huracanrana. The red-hot crowd rose to its feet in appreciation, once again chanting "TNA! TNA! TNA!"

So far, the match had been largely a high-flying affair. Now it was time for Joe to bring out his ground game.

After backdropping Styles out of the ring, Daniels decided to take Joe on at his own game. It would be a mistake. Daniels swatted Joe with a series of disrespectful open-handed slaps to the head. Joe exploded with stiff open-handed blows of his own. Daniels turtled and eventually found himself in the Coquina Clutch in the middle of the ring. Daniels, with Joe's legs wrapped around him, had nowhere to go. Joe was seconds away from victory.

Sensing that Joe was on the verge of taking home the X Division title, Styles ascended to the top rope. He had to break the hold. He could have done so with a kick or a flying elbow, but, realizing that he was on the biggest stage of his career, he knew that he'd have to do it in the way only A. J. Styles could. Leaping off the top strand, Styles twisted through the air like a whirlwind, smacking down on Joe and Daniels with a spectacular Spiral Tap. As fans cheered, all three wrestlers laid prone in the ring.

"As you look around the Impact! Zone," commented Mike Tenay, proudly, "you see everybody on their feet. They sense and they know that they're watching something very special!"

As the crowd joined in unison cheering, "This is awesome! This is awesome!" Joe knocked Styles down with vicious single-legged dropkick and followed up with a heavy senton back splash for a close two-count. A frustrated Joe was then stunned with a well-executed Death Valley driver by Daniels, who also garnered a two-count.

This back-and-forth, nonstop battle continued as Daniels and Styles exchanged fisticuffs on the arena floor. A seemingly incapacitated Joe rose to his feet and came charging toward the ropes. The 290-pounder leapt over the top rope and took out both Daniels and Styles with a corkscrew suicide dive. A nearly hoarse crowd once again shouted!

"For those of you who are watching this right now at home," barked color commentator West, "I want you to think how lucky you are—you're seeing one of the greatest matches in the history of wrestling!"

The match never slowed. Joe double-backdropped Daniels and Styles from the top rope. Daniels executed a spinning Tiger Bomb on Styles. Joe blasted Styles with his devastating Muscle Buster. Daniel flew through the air and crashed down on him with the BME: the "Best Moonsault Ever." Styles flipped from the second rope and hit an inverted DDT. Styles lifted the nearly 300-pound Samoan Submission Machine in a torture rack and slammed him to the mat. Styles even hit the Styles clash on Daniels. No man could score the pinfall or make another submit.

In the closing moments of the match, Joe was hurled outside the ring. Styles and Daniels swapped right hands, and Styles gained the advantage. After poking Styles in the eye, the champion hooked Styles in a double-arm suplex position—always the set-up for the Angel's Wings facebuster. Styles fought the hold, backdropping Daniels. Holding onto The Fallen Angel's arms, Styles bridged out and scored the match-ending pinfall at 22:50.

Styles was now five-time X Division champion. But more importantly, he had played a large role in TNA's finest hour as a wrestling promotion.

Today, Styles looks back on this match with fondness. "It was probably my best match," he remarks. "And it was so close to being the best match ever in wrestling, if you ask me."

"I think after the first year I realized that all the rumors saying that TNA's not going to make it, I let them go in one ear and out the other," Styles comments. "I'll believe that it's not gonna last when I see it. We're growing. And everybody keeps working hard."

Although major shareholder Panda Energy has lost $25 million from its investment in TNA so far, the league continues to live on and to play a major role in the lives of a number of young wrestlers, giving them shots at stardom.

MAT FACTS

NWA—Now You See It, Now You Don't

Upon its inception, TNA was a member of the National Wrestling Alliance with the company known as NWA-TNA. TNA was granted exclusive rights to both the NWA World Heavyweight Championship and the NWA World Tag Team Championship. TNA withdrew from the NWA in 2004 but was permitted to continue to use the championships until the NWA reneged on the agreement in May 2007.

Circling the Square

Although the promotion did at first use a WWE-style squared circle ring, TNA eventually became the first American promotion to exclusively use a hexagonal ring as opposed to the more conventional four-sided ring.

Rules of the Game

TNA employs the unconventional rule that a championship can change hands as the result of a disqualification or count out. In addition, two separate entrance ramps are used for heels and babyfaces.

New Exposure

Although TNA began by running shows available exclusively on pay-per-view, it soon achieved enough notoriety to earn a slot on free television. Its program, christened *TNA Impact!* premiered on June 4, 2004, on Fox Sports Net. *Impact!* soon replaced the weekly pay-per-views, and the company began broadcasting monthly pay-per-views as the main source of revenue. Unfortunately, the Fox contract was not renewed one year later as the show garnered consistently low ratings. This left TNA with no television deal other than the monthly pay-per-views, so on July 1, 2005, TNA turned to broadcasting *Impact!* from their official website, while seeking a new television outlet. Once again, TNA's future was in jeopardy. TNA would finally secure a deal with Spike TV and air its first episode on October 1, 2005. Since the move, the hour long *Impact!* show achieved considerably higher ratings and was moved twice, now having a primetime slot on Thursdays. The move to a two-hour format should happen by the end of 2007 and should help TNA expand its roster and build more stars.

Apart from their weekly shows, TNA has also starting running semi-regular house shows and expanded into other areas with the development of a video game with Midway Games, titled *TNA Impact!,* scheduled for release in 2008. In April 2006, TNA announced a partnership with YouTube that would see TNA supply YouTube with exclusive video content, leading to the production of Internet shows. In January 2007, TNA's mobile content deal with New Motion, Inc. led to the introduction of TNA Mobile and mobile fan voting.

Notes on Sources

The many DVDs, books and magazines and the wealth of clips of old matches on YouTube.com which I relied upon in the preparation of this book are too numerous to cite here. I nevertheless offer a few important books below. I also owe much to the UK-based monthly, *PowerSlam*. This book could never have been written without this wonderful publication.

Flair, Ric (and Keith Elliot Greenberg). *To Be The Man*. WWE Books, 2004.

Foley, Mick. *Have a Nice Day: A Tale of Blood and Sweatsocks*. HarperEntertainment, 1999.

Hogan, Hulk. *Hollywood Hulk Hogan*. WWE Books, 2002.

Hornbaker, Tim. *National Wrestling Alliance: The Untold Story of the Monopoly that Strangled Professional Wrestling*. ECW Press, 2006.

Lovero, Thom. *The Rise and Fall of ECW: Extreme Championship Wrestling*. WWE Books, 2006.

Reynolds, R.D. and Bryan Alvarez. *The Death of WCW*. ECW Press, 2004.

Colin Burnett

Born and raised in Montreal, Colin is an avid filmgoer and reader and has been a loyal wrestling fan since he watched his first match in 1987. His most memorable experience came while attending the Jacques Rougeau retirement show at the Montreal Forum in 1994. For a sellout crowd of about 18,000 fans, Rougeau piledrove his former partner Pierre Carl Ouellette to victory. When he is not watching wrestling, he teaches and studies film, paints and is a sucker for dark Belgian ale. Currently Colin is completing a PhD in communication arts.